"*Surrendered and Untamed* reaches into the depths of the human soul, taking an honest and refreshing look at what it means to have a personal relationship with the living God. Jason confronts 'religiosity' and brings Christianity back to the lifestyle Jesus set before His disciples of radical love and extreme faith. This book will renew your passion for the type of radical Christianity needed in the world today."

—**James Krechnyak Jr.**, church planter, Ireland; author, *Through the Wilderness* and *Living the Dream*

"Beautiful and thought provoking, but more than that . . . *Surrendered and Untamed* will unleash in you the desire to boldly go where you were destined to go and achieve the dreams God planted in your heart even against seemingly impossible odds. It will give you the awareness that Jesus is with you every step along the journey of life."

—**Julia Loren**, author, *When God Says Yes: His Promise & Provision When You Need It Most*

"I read it, loved it, laughed with it, and cried in it. My prayer is that God would find on earth not a generation of the selfish and comfortable, the independent and domesticated, but a generation of the totally surrendered and untamed. May I be one of them."

—**Mika Yrjola**, senior pastor, Canberra International Church

"Forty years ago, *The Edge of Adventure* by Keith Miller and Bruce Larson stood on top of the Christian bestseller list. The authors said one of the chief marks of emotional and spiritual health is a willingness to take risk. Well, a generation later comes *Surrendered and Untamed*. Jason Clark, Joel Clark, and Mark Batterson are living the adventure, taking bold risks, pushing every envelope, all in search of the story—the story of God's inbreaking, Christ's transforming, the .... work in their lives and in the lives of those around them. Consider yourself warned, your life will become less boring just for reading this!"

—**Jack Haberer**, editor, *Presbyterian Outlook*; author, *GodViews* and *Living the Presence of the Spirit*

"Jason Clark is a man sent from God. He has been wired to help us see aspects of God that we need to see, but that we may not have seen on our own. Like the apostle John, he urgently declares what he has both seen and heard. *Surrendered and Untamed* is his declaration, and reading it is an adventure. Hang on—this will stretch you."

—**Dick Grout**, director of music, Elim Bible Institute

Surrendered *and* Untamed

A Field Guide for the Vagabond Believer

Jason Clark

BakerBooks

a division of Baker Publishing Group
Grand Rapids, Michigan

Published by Baker Books
a division of Baker Publishing Group
P.O. Box 6287, Grand Rapids, MI 49516-6287
www.bakerbooks.com

Printed in the United States of America

Library of Congress Cataloging-in-Publication Data
Clark, Jason, 1974–
    Surrendered and untamed : a field guide for the vagabond believer / Jason
Clark.
        p.   cm.
    Includes bibliographical references (p.   ).
    ISBN 978-0-8010-1376-8 (pbk.)
    1. Christian life. I. Title.
BV4501.3.C523 2011
248.4—dc22   2010043419

Published in association with the literary agency of Alive Communications, Inc., 7680 Goddard Street, Suite 200, Colorado Springs, CO 80920, www.alivecommunications.com.

Permissions for lyrics on page 189.

11   12   13   14   15   16   17   7   6   5   4   3   2   1

This book is for my wife
Karen
and my kids,
Madeleine True,
Ethan Wilde,
and Eva Blaze.

I'm so loving living
surrendered and untamed
with you guys!

Contents

Foreword

Two thousand years ago Jesus birthed the most catalytic revolution of all time. Since then, this redemptive revolution has been joined by revolutionaries who will accept nothing less than an authentic relationship with that same Jesus. This revolution is defined by willing adventurers who live wholly surrendered to Christ and passionately untamed in their pursuit of His glory.

As we surrender to God, we enjoy the incredible freedom to live an untamed life—wild after God's mission in the world. It's our surrender that leads us into the presence of God, and it's these God encounters that define and release us into an untamed existence. And this existence is available to every believer! It is found in the promise Jesus made before He ascended, a promise that was first realized in the Upper Room. A promise of a Spirit-led life, a Spirit-breathed life, a life of seeing where the Father moves and moving with Him.

"I tell you the truth, anyone who has faith in me will do what I have been doing. He will do even greater things than these," Jesus tells us.[1] In fact, Jesus's whole message on earth points to a "greater works than these" lifestyle. His words are an open invitation to live a life marked by the power and presence of God. But I must warn you: this is not an invitation to an easy life. Quite the opposite. There is great risk involved in following Jesus. Will you believe in God enough to take this risk? This central question reverberates throughout Jason's book.

God gave us the promise of a Spirit-led life, and yet sometimes holding onto that promise can be so hard. There is a difference between making a living and making a life. So many people settle for the former. God calls us to the latter. And I believe this book will help you lay claim to the abundant life Jesus promised.

Our lives must be rooted in a firm faith that God is always good, that He is bigger than everything else, that He has all authority, and that He fulfills all He says He will.

Paul said, "If God is for us, who can be against us? He who did not spare his own Son, but gave him up for us all—how will he not also, along with him, graciously give us all things?"[2] That is our birthright. And it ought to fill every child of God with a sense of destiny. The revolution has started. The invitation has been extended.

Are you in?

—Mark Batterson

Introduction

It was a crisp, sunny fall afternoon in 2006, one of those days that inspires the imagination. Joel was visiting us from South Africa and was dreaming out load about an idea he had as we relaxed in our living room.

"So, what do you think?"

"I think it's amazing, an awesome opportunity!" I said.

He leaned toward me. "But do you want to do it?"

Joel had just signed on to film a documentary of his good friend Alex Harris on a 692-mile trek to the South Pole. Alex is a world-renowned South African explorer—a guy I had heard a lot about in the past years as he and Joel had become pretty close. When Joel lived in Johannesburg, he used to meet weekly with Alex to connect and pray.

Alex was always doing something crazy cool, like summiting Everest or Adventure Racing (100,000 kilometers by mountain bike, cross country running, climbing, paddling, and probably some crawling). And Joel was always telling me a new story, like when he and Alex rappelled a waterfall or went caving. Now they were heading to Antarctica together. It was going to be amazing, and I was thrilled for him and slightly envious. I wanted to go with them, but it would cost $30,000 per person and I had just bought a minivan.

But Joel wasn't inviting me to go, not this time; he was inviting me to partner with him on a project that was bigger than anything I had ever dreamed of. While he was in Antarctica, he also wanted to film an inspiring devotional to encourage believers to love bigger, dream grander, and ultimately know a greater revelation of God. Joel wanted to call it *Surrendered & Untamed*, and he wanted me to write the book.

A year earlier I had recorded an album by the same title. This one album birthed the book you hold in your hands, a DVD, and the participant's guide for the DVD.

As you get into the book, you will notice lyrics below the headings. These are my song lyrics, most of which are from the *Surrendered & Untamed* album.

The S&U message is pretty simple: to the extent that we surrender our lives to God, we are free to live untamed. Living untamed means that we are free to chase down dreams, free to believe and wildly step out in risk. Essentially, it is our surrender that releases us into this freedom. And it is this freedom that allows us to fully live out the promises God has placed within every one of us.

Joel and my wife Karen carried on their conversation. The idea that God might want me to write a book started me laughing, which interrupted Joel and Karen's conversation. They both looked at me.

"What?" they asked in unison.

"I'll write the book," I said, smiling.

They were smiling too but they didn't get the joke. I laughed again.

I ask God questions all the time. "God, should I start this company? Should I go on that trip? Should I eat these Doritos? Will the Buffalo Bills ever win a Super Bowl?" Very rarely does He answer in such a real and immediate way. I'm not sure He cares about the Doritos and I've often questioned whether or not He's a Bills fan. But when it came to writing, I think He knew I would need a big yes, because it would take the next four years and many of the truths I would write I hadn't fully experienced yet.

And that's what this book is—revelations from a vagabond believer, stories of a fledgling revivalist, the journaling of a fellow traveler learning to believe in greater measure.

On this journey I am learning that we all have a one-of-a-kind promise from God: His kingdom within us. This promise is unique to every individual, is discovered in our dreams, and lives in our hearts. And His promises are greater than anything we could ask or imagine. I haven't always fully known what my promise looks like, but if I'm willing to surrender—my heart for His—I get to engage and experience all His heart offers. And that's what untamed living is all about—coalescing my promise with His purpose.

I didn't go with Alex and Joel to Antarctica. I had my own landscape to navigate. This book isn't about Alex or the South Pole, although the message is the same. This is my journaled journey toward learning how to live absolutely Surrendered and radically Untamed. The book doesn't guarantee long life or comfort. It doesn't have any formulas in it on how to be happy or how to make a quick buck. It's meant to encourage you on your journey; to release you into greater freedom that you might begin to dream, believe, and engage the unique promises of God for your life.

God bless your journey!

1

The Promise

The Polar Express

> *Maybe you got tired of living stale*
> *Playing safe while all your ships set off to sail*

I was sitting in the theatre beside a three-year-old boy named Ethan Wilde. Ethan is my son. We were about to watch *The Polar Express*. I was a little distracted because we had just moved to North Carolina. We were pretty sure God had asked us to. Pretty sure. We had spent our savings and were now digging into our "good credit." We were beyond strapped, and spending eight bucks for the afternoon matinee caused that voice in my head to say, *Are you crazy?*

A thirty-year-old man with a wife and two kids isn't usually 100 percent certain of much, but I was about 97 percent sure I was to spend all my time and resources birthing a ministry.

I would later find out that this was a lifestyle and that my true ministry was simply believing God. He had told me to believe, to stay the course. But as the money flew out of our bank account, I was more than worried. I was scared.

Dave Ramsey's evaluation would have been . . . uh, financial suicide. Now, I know Dave Ramsey has saved many people from financial ruin. But this was between me and another Savior; it had nothing to do with financial responsibility. This was about irresponsible, unsound, downright foolish obedience. I'll return to this a little later. . . .

Back to *The Polar Express*. If you haven't seen it, try to; it's wonderful. It's about a young boy who, while growing up, loses his ability to believe in God—I mean Santa Claus. Fortunately, Jesus, the Holy Spirit, and God—I mean three variations of Tom Hanks—band together to guide the boy back into believing. I realize that sounds confusing, but stick with me.

It's Christmas Eve and instead of dreaming of the best day of the year, the boy is in his bedroom agonizing over the universal question: Does God . . . sorry, I mean Santa Claus . . . really exist? He used to believe, but now in the mind of this blossoming adult, a fat, bearded, jolly man delivering presents to the entire world's population in one night seems impossible. Add in flying reindeer, elves, a North Pole toy factory—it all seems completely foolish. The boy is in danger of becoming a realist.

And then a deep rumbling. It grows louder until it fills his room and even jumps out into our theatre seats. Like an earthquake, it shakes and rattles his shelf of sports trophies. The boy crawls over to his window, peers out and what to his wondering eyes should appear? An enormous train decked in his front yard.

Dressed in his pajamas and rubber rain boots, he cautiously walks out to the train and meets Jesus . . . I'm sorry, I mean a train conductor played by Tom Hanks. The conductor says, "Well . . . are you coming?"

That's a question worth remembering.

16

This amazes the boy. He really wants to get on the train, but at the same time, the idea terrifies him. Finally, as the train begins to inch forward, his heart wins out and he takes the outstretched hand of the conductor.

And so the journey begins, a grand adventure filled with mountaintops and frozen lakes and howling wolves and dancing waiters balancing hot chocolate. It's exciting and dangerous all at the same time. Along the way the boy meets the Holy Spirit . . . I'm sorry, I mean a ghost who oddly resembles Tom Hanks.

After several breathtaking moments, the train reaches its destination—the North Pole. There are elves everywhere, and music, dancing, and singing. It is truly a magical place. I'd like to go there someday.

Everyone is awaiting Santa's arrival, which signals the official start of Christmas. The elves are singing Christmas songs. Some are whispering, "Is he here?" and some are yelling, "Do you see him?" The anticipation is almost unbearable.

The reindeer harnessed to Santa's sleigh are going wild! Their master is coming! They can sense it! The sleigh bells are ringing and all who believe in Santa can hear them, their pristine crystal tones adding to the beautiful, chaotic anticipation. The children that made the journey are there too. The air is electric.

And then there is the boy. He had all but decided that Santa is not real and yet wants—with his whole heart—to be wrong. Surrounded by a sea of believers, the boy dares to hope; in fact, hope is everywhere, and it's contagious.

A slow hush falls on the crowd, and all eyes become focused on a building at the end of the square. The doors burst open. There is a bright light and within the doorframe a silhouette. Suddenly the whole square erupts. "There he is!" shouts an elf. "I see him!" says one of the girls, but the boy, pressed by the crowd, can't see and still can't hear the sleigh bells. Why can't he hear? Desperate, he jumps and presses his way through the sea of elves to the front. And then, there He is, God . . . I'm sorry, I mean Santa Claus, who is also played by Tom Hanks. . . .

Suddenly the boy hears everything: the bells, the worshiping elves, the celebrating kids, the dancing reindeer. And I'm sitting beside my son, and I'm desperately trying to hide my face from the little girl next to me. Why? 'Cause I'm bawling my eyes out and whispering, "I believe, I believe, I believe . . . I love You, Lord, and I believe . . ."

I've been given a promise from God. But sometimes holding on to it can be rather difficult. Life moves along, things happen; the world is a very busy and noisy place. It's easy to wake up one day and find you're just not sure anymore. Believing has become a lost art and the promise has become a mountain that seems unscalable. In fact, it has often seemed, the harder I try to summit, the farther the peak is from me. But I'm convinced that the "God-lived life" is one of learning *how* to believe. It's learning how to cling to God and keep His promises alive in your heart.

In the movie it took the conductor, the ghost, and Santa working together to woo the child. One man played all three characters, a trinity working in unison, until ultimately the boy made the decision to believe. The boy's heart had wanted to believe from the very start. And that desire was enough to push him into the perilous journey.

Consider the possibility that God is asking you the very same question: *Well . . . are you coming?*

The Gas Attendant

> *Up and away, up in a hope-filled night*
> *You climbed away, awake for the first time*

I got my first job at the Co-Op. A mini Walmart of sorts, it even had a gas station in the parking lot. Lucky for me. My dad had driven me there to apply and had assured Bill, the manager, that I could be trusted. I explained to Bill how I could easily ride my ten-speed to work, how it made "perfect sense" . . . and so at the age of fifteen for $5.50 an hour Canadian, I became a gas attendant.

I remember this job well: cold nights where I was forced to either stand outside and freeze or sit in the 5′ x 10′ heated cubicle with my two pot-smoking co-workers. They were bright fellas for potheads and to my knowledge never got caught smoking while on the job.

Bill the manager was anything but patient. This was probably due to the fact that he was a middle-aged man managing pot-smoking teenagers pumping gas. He was almost always mad at someone or something; he coped by screaming. So when the sweet old lady came in to fill up her brand-new Cadillac and asked me to top off her oil, I didn't want to bother Bill with silly questions such as "Where does the oil go?" or "How much is too much?" I did what any fifteen-year-old would do. I guessed.

About a half hour later, the sweet old lady was back and she seemed to be having steering problems. "I just don't understand it," she said. "The steering wheel is very hard to turn and it only started happening after I got gas." I said what any fifteen-year-old would say: "It must be bad gas."

One would think that my gas attendant career was over before it had even been given a fighting chance. But four years later I was again being driven by my dad to apply for a job as a gas attendant. This time I lived just south of Rochester, New York. I was a freshman attending Bible college.

I went to Bible college, not seminary. I feel I must make this absolutely clear, because several seminary graduates have felt duty bound to inform me of the differences between the two. So we're clear, right? A Bible college does not a seminary make.

I went to Bible college because that's where I thought I'd find "it." You see, at the age of five, kneeling at the coffee table one sunny Tuesday afternoon with my mom, I asked Jesus to come into my heart. And Jesus did. Then God did something that still blows me away: He made me a promise. God—the One who made heaven and earth—made me a promise. I eventually would discover that it was just the first of many to come, but it also was the most profound. On that Tuesday long ago, God promised He would always be with me—that His presence would always be in me. And I believed Him. It was just a small believing at first, but it was enough. I trusted that life was good and God's presence would lead to great things, a life of adventure marked by the miraculous.

I have since heard the promise referred to as *destiny* or *purpose*. That's fine. I believe it's those things. But I like the word *promise* so much more. It implies that I'm not the only one involved in its fulfillment. It suggests that there is more to it than hard work and chance. It hints at relationship.

Through the years this promise haunted me like a lovely ghost. I would encounter it in a song or in a book. I'd dream it or see it in a movie. I even heard it in sermons. It's been a gradual strengthening—a realization of who God is, that He lives in me and that He is good. He is always good.

Now back to Bible college, pumping gas as a job for the second time.

In January, in upstate New York, it's dark by 5:00 p.m. and below freezing by 5:30. On this—my first night at the job—it was about five degrees with a windchill somewhere in the minus ten department. My new co-worker and I were warming up inside our little 5′ x 10′ heated cubicle (no pot this time) as a black Volvo pulled up to the pump. I had filled up the last ten cars and was positive it wasn't my turn, but my co-worker said, "You go ahead and get this one. That way we can be sure you know what you're doing."

I looked at him just long enough to let him know what we both already knew—he was an idiot—and then headed out into the frozen night, my lungs immediately icing over. The lady in the car rolled her window down an inch and said, "Fill it up, please," and then quickly rolled it back up with a look of sympathy.

As I stomped my feet to keep them warm and wiped my nose with the back of my hand, I thought, "This sucks! But

God wants me here." OK, I'm not certain I thought the second part . . . OK, I probably didn't think the second part as I was freezing my tail off.

But I did think it later, in my bed while talking with God. I just knew He wanted me at this Bible college. I just knew He had a plan for me and this is where I would discover the grand adventure; where I would finally find the promised life of significance filled with love and beauty and probably a little fame too.

That pursuit is what kept me pumping gas in western New York on desperately cold nights in order to earn enough money to afford a Bible college education that later couldn't be compared to a seminary education. All this gas pumping was just a means to my end, my promise, "it."

The days turned to months and the months to years. Pumping gas became waiting tables, became playing in a band, became working in construction, became leading worship at a church. And in the pursuit I grew weary. "How many more cars do I have to fill up, Lord?" "How many more Bible classes?" "How many more occupations?" "How much longer must I chase 'it'"?

Several years ago, God and I had a profound conversation. Late one night after Karen and the kids were in bed, God asked me a question. "Do you trust Me?" I thought for a moment. Finally, I said, "Yes, Lord." He responded, "Then believe."

From that moment, my perspective on life has undergone a radical shifting. All that I encountered over the first ten years of my adult life, including the jobs I just mentioned, were experienced while pursuing my promise—"it." I believed they were things I had to go through to reach my goal. But since that conversation with God, I have begun to live in the revelation that I was not born into His Kingdom to chase the promise but to chase the Promise Giver.

I am no longer chasing an ever-elusive promise but embracing it. I'm no longer waiting for my story to begin; I'm smack in the middle of it.

In the beginning God dreamed and a world was born. A love story began. Since the beginning of this story, the all-powerful Creator of the heavens and the earth has pursued humankind, has loved us, died for us, and invited us to live within the context of His love. From day one, God has purposed man to rule and reign with Him over the earth. And there has always been one question that God has asked of us. It's echoed down the corridors of history:

Will you believe?

Or as Tom Hanks said: *Well . . . are you coming?*

The Eternal Optimist

I've felt a sense of urgency
A lion come alive in me, in revelation of Your
*   love*

The little boy in *The Polar Express*, the one who stopped believing? I identify with him. Yeah, that was me, my story. Hi, my name is Jason and I'm a recovering realist.

I chased the promise for so long, I lost sight of the Promise Giver. Somewhere along the way I had stopped believing. I became exhausted, unmotivated, and unsure, where once I had been positive. Life became random and dull. In one sense I still did what I thought God had created me to do, but it no longer held meaning. I started filtering every experience through an attitude of hopelessness, until every bump in the road was expected, while every triumph was fleeting. The fact was, as a realist, I had begun living a life where the glass was neither half full nor half empty. It was just . . . half.

But now I'm putting all my money on the Promise Giver and following Him where He leads me, like moving my family to North Carolina and financially disappointing Dave Ramsey. I have made a decision that I am going to be a believer, whether it looks good or not, whether it feels good or not. I have made a decision to say *yes*. It's really the only way to continue moving forward in my own story. It's also the only way to live the promise, to experience life, immense joy, and fulfillment. However, I must warn you, it's also an open invitation to trials and criticism, often from the Christian community.

I can't explain all this from a realist perspective; it's just not there. I'm afraid realism is living in the kingdom of man. While realism can often appear to be practical, respectable, and wise, it's simply unbelief. In fact, I think that realism is just a socially accepted form of pessimism. Realism says, "If you don't have the money, God must not be in it. . . . If you're sick, it must be God's will—maybe He is trying to teach you something. . . . If you're poor, get a job! . . . If you want to minister, go to Bible college or seminary. . . . If you're offending someone's sensibilities, then stop." Basically, whatever you do, be careful or you may come out looking like an idiot. In short, if at all possible, avoid risk. We must protect what God gave us; we need to be responsible and careful regarding our "Christian walk." We need to be respectable, nice, and tame. And oh yeah, did I mention frustrated, fed up, and bored out of our minds?! And don't forget aimless, empty, and miserable.

Believing is living in the kingdom of God. Believing inspires action, births revelation, and yields miracles. A realist would see a blind man and say he can't see, end of story. But when Jesus came to earth, the blind saw, the lame walked, the deaf heard, Lazarus died twice, and Jesus told death, "Thanks, but no!" From what I can tell, God is not a realist. He is the Eternal Optimist and He has called all of us to be eternally optimistic with Him.

Believing is keeping your eye on the prize; it's forward living, faith in motion. Belief is good, but for it to grow, it needs to be nurtured by a believing lifestyle. "I tell you the truth, anyone who has faith in me will do what I have been

23

doing. He will do even greater things than these."[1] Jesus's whole message on earth points to a "greater works than these" lifestyle. Believing in Him is living in that promise.

The promise—your promise and mine—is one of a Spirit-led life, a Spirit-breathed life, a life of seeing where the Father moves and moving with Him.

What does this greater-works promise look like for me? Well, I can't see all of it, but I'm learning that it lives in my heart and can be found in my dreams—particularly the dreams that most excite and most terrify me. I also am learning that the only way to see more of it, to engage it, is to develop a believing heart.

We live in a culture that has deified the mind. Yes, God gave us brains, but the thinking mind is never to replace the believing heart. They work in tandem, but the heart must come first. Or as a friend of mine says, we too often put the course before the heart. Jesus lives in our hearts. Believing often doesn't add up in the mind, as something you can see. But faith, after all, is the essence of things unseen.[2]

I'm afraid I would still be a realist today if not for the wild yearning in my heart to want more, to continue to dream. And God's wild yearning for me. God in His grace and faithfulness has intervened in some very godlike ways. He's used pot-smoking co-workers, freezing cold temperatures, and even Bible college to bring me along. Then there are also those wild believers who have affected my life—men and women who modeled godly optimism by living lives marked by the dangerous favor of God. Some of them have been flesh and blood, like my dad and my wife Karen and my son, Ethan. Others have been enfleshed in stories, like God-the-conductor-Tom-Hanks on a silver screen asking "the" question—

Well . . . are you coming?

2

He Loves Me Best

God is always speaking . . . to me, and to you as well. I've learned that I can hear His voice through the Bible, in nature, by way of my friends, family, and elders. He speaks through some of my favorite authors. I've found Him in songs and movies. I'm also learning that often that "gentle whisper" in my heart is God.

This may be a revolutionary concept to you—that the Creator of the world is speaking to each and every one of us, every day, all the time. What makes it even more amazing is, regardless of how the message is delivered, God is always saying the same thing: "I love you," followed by one question, "Do you believe Me?"

Sinbad, Seacrest, and Paper Cuts

There is a love beyond understanding
There is a grace that consumes

I was already tired and we were only 7 hours into a 33-hour trip. My dad and I were on our way to China to look at some business opportunities. We left Charlotte, North Carolina, in the afternoon. Why start a 33-hour trip in the afternoon? I don't know, and neither did the lady at the airline counter. When I asked her, she looked annoyed and said, "That's just how they do it."

We were standing in LAX, and though I was tired, I was excited as well. You see, last time I went through LAX, I got to meet Sinbad. Well, I didn't actually meet him, more like saw him—practically the same thing. He was in line to check his luggage.

He really is a funny guy. He didn't do anything funny while I was watching him, which was a little disappointing, but I imagine it's hard to be funny all the time. It *was* early and everyone knows it's easier to be funny later in the day. I bet he's hilarious after lunch.

So it gets better, because after I saw Sinbad, I saw Ryan Seacrest, who hosts *American Idol*. How cool is that? I actually did meet him; we sat in first class together.

I know what you are thinking. I'm that rich snob who sits in first class and looks down his nose at all the second-class people, the saps headed to coach.

Well, maybe I am. Maybe I like getting to go into the plane first. Maybe I enjoy sitting Indian style in my comfortable leather seat while the second-class rabble are trotted through first class. Maybe I like having a curtain separate me from the cacophony of noises and smells wafting off the masses that sit in second class. Maybe I enjoy a nice Chardonnay while speaking in high English with the cream of the world citizenry.

Or maybe the flight was overbooked and I got bumped to first class.

For that one glorious day I was cultured and civilized and just an all-around better person. That was the day I flew like a king!

26

So I sat in first class and Ryan and I discussed the last show of the season and the new *American Idol*. He was very polite, a nice fella. And I think I held my own; that is to say, I don't think he knew I didn't belong there—in first class.

But I digress. Back to my China trip.

I was excited about this trip because of the possibility of seeing someone famous but also because I love to travel and we were going to places I had never been.

The airport in LA was crowded. We were standing in line with about two hundred people in front of us, plus the thousands of others who filled our little universe known as Terminal Two. Surrounded by the huddled masses, I began to have one of those feelings that I think everyone experiences from time to time. I felt small. With thousands of people moving through that section of the airport every five minutes and the knowledge that we were about to go to a country with a population of over a billion, I suddenly felt . . . insignificant.

I wonder if Sinbad ever feels insignificant? Probably not . . . I guess.

We had about an hour wait to get through customs and check our bags for the international flight. While I was standing there feeling "small," I noticed the girl in front of me. She was standing with her back to me, her arms crossed. I could just see the tips of the fingers on her left hand. I noticed that her index finger had a tiny cut. It was a little inflamed and looked like it could be irritated, but it was nothing serious, just a paper cut. Suddenly I felt the presence of God as if He was standing right next to me. Then He said to my heart, "I was there when that happened, I felt that."

Now as I mentioned earlier, God is always speaking and sometimes He says the strangest things. This seemed to me to be one of those times. So I responded to God in my heart.

"God, I can't possibly understand this, my mind can't begin to grasp it. I am just a spec in the universe, a blink of the eye

27

in light of eternity." As I looked around at the thousands of people, I became overwhelmed.

"God, how many paper cuts are in this place? How many people are here with problems deeper than paper cuts? What would possess You to even point out a small, insignificant paper cut? How is it possible for me to understand this, God?"

Then God said to my heart, "It's not about your understanding, it's about your believing—believing the absolute goodness that is My love. Do you believe Me?"

At that moment I got a glimpse of God's heart of love, and it overwhelmed me. I could barely compose myself. I was awed by the revelation that His love for the world included paper cuts. To be fair, I'm not sure I believed Him. To be honest, I absolutely wanted too.

So I said in my heart, "Yes, God, I choose to believe. Now please show me how."

Revelation

Let me find my joy complete
Let me see, oh love, be my sweet witness

Let me tell you how it is between my wife and me.

We could be driving down the road or sitting on the couch watching *The Office* when suddenly I am gripped with a revelation of how amazing Karen is. I will remember how she was so patient with our kids earlier in the day, or how she just made me coffee and I didn't even ask for it and it was the perfect mix of coffee, cream, and sugar. Or how stunning the back of her neck is.

I will turn to her and say that simple universal phrase—"I love you"—to which she always responds, "I love you too, gorgeous."

But sometimes in these unveiled moments I'll stop what I'm doing and say, "Karen, I'm feeling it right now! At this exact moment I am having a revelation of my love for you! My heart, mind, and soul are loving you right now."

"Right this instant?" she asks, her eyes bright.

"Yes, this exact moment."

"Wow." She smiles. "Now I'm feeling it too!"

Often this interaction is followed by an encounter. . . . That is to say, there might be a shared smile or a hug, a kiss, or—

Well, that's none of your business.

I believe revelation, in the context of a love relationship, always leads to a greater love encounter, a greater intimacy. In fact, that's the whole point of revelation. Karen and I have been married fifteen years. We know that we love each other, we say it all the time, we decide to all the time. But these moments of revelation are priceless. They are birthed of a pure surrender one to another, where everything in the universe aligns and our hearts, minds, and souls experience the encounter. In these moments, nothing else matters! In these moments, the truth of our love is purely revealed and is always deepened.

I am convinced that when it comes to our relationship with God, revelation is meant to lead to a greater encounter. Revelation means "to remove the veil"; it's always about knowing in greater measure the love of God. I am also convinced that there is always more.

He Loves Me Best

Sweet love, come, darling, the air is alive,
The time is ripe for you and me

Do you know who wrote the gospel of John? John did—I looked it up. Do you know that three times in the gospel of John, he refers to himself in third person? Each time this is revealed as "the *one* Jesus loved." It's almost as if John is saying "Jesus loved me best."

29

Think about this. If anyone knew God's love, it would be the disciples. John, being one of the twelve, lived with Jesus for three years. They did life together; they laughed, cried, ate, walked, and prayed together.

John was there for the miracles, when Jesus healed, delivered, forgave, restored, and made more food out of less. John was there when Jesus was moved with compassion and poured Himself out to the lost, weak, blind, deaf, and lame. Whatever the need, John watched Jesus meet it.

John was also around when Jesus was whipped and beaten, spit upon and cursed. He was there when Jesus was spread out, nailed to, and then hung on a cross—love in human form giving up His life for humankind.

And John was there after the resurrection, when Jesus displayed His nail-scarred hands and feet. He witnessed love ascend to heaven and experienced love again when it descended in the form of the Holy Spirit. If anyone knew what love looked like, it was John.

And John, the guy who knew intimately what love looked like and felt like and acted like, goes on to write about himself as "the *one* Jesus loved."

As far as John was concerned, he was Jesus's favorite. Jesus loved him best.

Somehow John's relationship with Jesus nurtured the most profound revelation a person can possess. John knew God's love as an intimate, one-of-a-kind love. I believe that revelation is available to you and me.

To know I am "the *one* He loves" is my heart's truest desire, and I would like to suggest that it's yours as well.

So I am learning to believe Him when He says, "I love you." In fact it's become my life's one true ambition—that I could say regarding myself, "I am the *one* He loves." And as I keep choosing to believe Him, I have come to realize that it is the most important thing I will ever believe.

Though I have but the smallest sliver of understanding, in my heart of hearts, where I continue to know His love in

30

greater measure, I am betting that I just might be His favorite; that He is especially fond of me, that He loves me best, that I am "the *one* He loves." I'd also wager that if you ask Him, He will tell you the same thing: He loves you best too.

The Puppy

Singing, oh my God, You are
Such a holy love, enough
And still I must have more

I was there with my four-year-old Ethan on the Virginia hilltop that crisp fall day. I sat on the trail edge with him in my lap, looking out on the valley of burnt oranges and brilliant reds. And I prayed with him when he asked Jesus into his heart. It is one of my favorite memories.

Ethan isn't an overly expressive boy—except when scoring touchdowns. He is shy and quiet around strangers. I think it comes from his Canadian Anglo-Saxon roots. It's the same excuse I use for not dancing in public. Anyway, for the two years following Ethan's salvation prayer, he was reserved. That is to say, his faith was a private one. When it came to life, he was loud at Lego Star Wars and flag football. But when it came to praying, he was beyond quiet—he had nothing to say.

Ethan didn't like to pray. Not at the supper table, not at bedtime, not in the morning, "not in a box, not with a fox, not in a house, not with a mouse,"[1] and certainly not at church. He was shy. He was embarrassed. He did his best to give the impression of disinterest. I was facing a parent's conundrum. I wanted my son to learn how to pray, but I wasn't certain how to make it happen. I had been trying to find a way to encourage him, not for form or religious expression, but for relationship—that he might encounter God's love through prayer.

To embrace our promise, we must walk in close relationship with God, and one of the ways this happens is through our prayer life. Prayer is one of the ways we learn how to hear God. This hearing is absolutely essential. So I was intent on my son not just knowing about God but knowing and being known by God.

Several years ago on a Saturday morning, two years after Ethan's salvation experience, our kids came into the bedroom and jumped in bed with us. After the customary "good morning" and "how did you sleep?" my daughter Maddy told a story about a friend of hers who just got a puppy.

As a parent of children without a puppy, this is dangerous territory. But before I could say anything to defuse the situation, Karen blurted out, "It would be fun to get a puppy!"

That's all it took.

Maddy heard a positive comment about a dog, and the little fire we had spent years squelching immediately ignited into a raging inferno. "We should get one! I want a puppy sooo bad!"

Ethan chimed in, "Me too, it would be so cool!"

I looked at Karen incredulously and then did my best to give her the evil eye. She just smiled.

The rest of the morning was spent discussing all the reasons we couldn't get a dog right now.

As I got out of bed I said, "Your sister Eva is too little." Maddy said, "She's almost two, Dad, and then she will be three!"

As I brushed my teeth, I garbled, "We don't have a fence." Maddy was ready for that one—"I will walk him every day, three times a day!" "Yeah, me too!" Ethan promised.

As I put my shoes on to go for my morning run, I said, "What about the poop—who's gonna pick it up?" I thought I had them on that one. Maddy didn't even hesitate, "We will, of course!"

When I got back from my run, Maddy and Ethan met me on the front porch. As I stretched, Maddy began explaining how they could get a bucket and a shovel and how her friend has a dog and they pick up the poop with bags.

I showered and dressed and found Maddy and Ethan waiting outside the bathroom door with drawings of them playing with the "beautiful puppy." "What's this one?" I asked Ethan. "In that picture I am wrestling with the puppy," he grinned. "And this one?" I asked as I took the second offering out of his hands. "In that picture I am sleeping with the puppy." He actually giggled, which if you are a parent you know is almost impossible to experience without joining in. I giggled with him and then realized I was dangerously close to being swayed by Maddy's sincere enthusiasm and Ethan's boyish charm.

I had to leave for a meeting. But before I left, I found Karen in her office and, with as much accusation as I could muster, said, "You started this!" She just smiled.

What I found when I got home blew my mind. Karen was on the computer, the kids were hovering around her. As soon as I walked in, the kids started yelling,

"Dad, come see, come see! It's the most cutest puppy ever!"

"Seriously?!" I said to Karen. She just smiled.

The Maddy-Ethan-persistent-spouse stuff continued all afternoon and evening. Karen just kept smiling.

Finally it was bedtime. I sat at the foot of Maddy's bed while she scratched my head, and Ethan sat on the floor with me. I told them a story about how, one time when I was younger, I went on a treasure hunt. I discovered a cave with a golden statue. The cave was booby trapped with poisonous arrows that shot out of the cave walls. And there was a huge pit that I had to use my whip to swing across.

And after I got the statue, the place started to cave in and a huge perfectly round boulder almost flattened me. I barely escaped the cave . . .

After my story, I prayed for both of them. Maddy wanted to raise the puppy discussion again, but I pulled that old dad trick—"I don't want to talk about it anymore until I have discussed it with your mom." Then I herded Ethan into his bedroom to tuck him in.

When I got there, he didn't want to talk about the story or even wrestle. He just wanted to discuss the puppy. I had planned on using the same tactic I'd used with Maddy, when God spoke to my heart. It was so beautiful I choked up.

"Jason, I love you. Do you believe Me?"

Suddenly I knew what God wanted me to do. While kneeling by Ethan's bed, I said, "Hey, buddy, let me ask you a serious question. How much do you think God loves you?"

He paused. "I don't know."

I asked another question. "Do you think God wants you to have a puppy?"

For a moment there was hope in his eyes. Then he got serious and again said, "I don't know."

I smiled and leaned in. "I want you to pray and ask God whether we should get a puppy. You and God talk for a while and then you tell me what He says. We will do whatever He tells you."

I could barely control myself emotionally as I said this to him. I already knew God's answer. You see, He loves my son with a love that rivals His love for me. I kissed Ethan on the forehead and said, "I want you to really talk with God and hear what He says. When you have heard from Him, come tell me."

Ethan looked at me, scrunched his brow and in a reverent tone said, "OK, Dad."

About twenty minutes later he walked downstairs. "Dad?"

"Yes?" I said.

"I think God wants us to get a puppy."

I nearly started crying again. My son and God were talking! "Are you sure?" I asked.

"I think so," Ethan said.

"Well, I think so too, but I want you to be sure. Go pray some more until you are sure."

Another twenty minutes or so passed and he came down again, this time grinning ear to ear.

"I'm sure!" he said.

"Me too. Let's get a puppy!"

Better than Oreos and Milk

Your heart be our compass,
To be known by Your love

What would our lives look like if we could answer the question God is always asking: "Do you believe that I love you?" What would life be like if we could somehow live in the revelation that the plans He has for us really are always good?[2] What kind of people would we become if we could somehow breathe in and out such authentic hope. How profound would our joy be to know this Jesus?

First John 4:8 says it best: "Whoever does not love does not know God, because God is love." God is love. The words "God" and "love" are interchangeable. His very nature is love. The very foundation of this universe is love.

You could read the famous wedding Scripture from 1 Corinthians 13 and replace the word *love* with *God*, like this—

> *God* is patient, *God* is kind. *He* does not envy, *He* does not boast, *He* is not proud. *He* is not rude, *He* is not self-seeking, *He* is not easily angered, *He* keeps no record of wrongs. *God* does not delight in evil but rejoices with the truth. *He* always protects, always trusts, always hopes, always perseveres.[3]

When you begin to realize that every God encounter is birthed from love, well, it changes everything else. Our ability to live surrendered and untamed, to engage our promise, is founded in an understanding that "I am the one He loves." It's from that revelation that everything else flows. Everything.

Here's the thing. I believe the whole point of revelation is to be changed by His love—to know His love that we might know more of His love, what I call "owning revelation."

Truth can be read about and discussed, but to own revelation requires some form of experience. "God loves you" can be nothing more than words. But engaging the words opens the door to the power of change.

God is love and each time I open myself to His love He reveals Himself to me in greater measure. It's a little scary, but in a very good way, kinda like when you first dipped your Oreos in milk but way better. I am learning that the more aware I am of how much He loves me, the greater access I have to the power of His love.

I am learning that the power of His love is life altering. It's my salvation, my redemption, and my provision. It's my strength, my joy, and my peace. God's love is an all-consuming fire that encompasses every particle of me—*if* I surrender, *if* I let it. Every need or question I have is answered in a greater revelation of His love.

I would like to suggest that a surrendered and untamed life begins when we believe that He loves us. In fact, I'm convinced that our promise is only embraced to the depth that we believe God when He tells us He loves us.

This isn't a "feel-good gospel" that I'm preaching; this is a feel-good, love-good, live-good, die-good, pray-good, give-good, suffer-good, praise-good Gospel. . . . It's all Good!

This isn't name-it-claim-it, this is about knowing-owning. This isn't about God giving us things, but about the revelation of God's love. This is about an understanding that He loves us as "the one," and regardless of our circumstances, His love is good, always.

Can you imagine if our hearts were like Ethan's when we prayed? Can you imagine if we could truly come to God with such sincere anticipation? I believe that if we knew His love, truly knew His love, we would never fear again. Sin wouldn't exist and nothing would be impossible. Though this full revelation may not take place until we reach heaven, I believe it's available to us here on earth now in greater measure than we could even ask or imagine.

The Creator of the universe has written us into the greatest love story of all time. He has invited us to believe, engage His love, and *become* love with Him.

So when I asked Jesus if He wanted me to pray for financial blessing, He said, "Yes." When I asked if He wanted me to pray for healing, He said, "Yes."

"Jesus, do you want us to have a puppy?" He said, "Yes." And smiled.

3

Monday Morning

My Biggest Fear

I'm walking, waiting for You
Where is it You're going to
I trust we'll get there in time

Several years ago, my dad, my brother Joel, and I joined a pickup hockey league—better known as a beer league. This is a group of men who get to act like boys for a couple hours, two nights a week. We loved it. It was the first time all three of us had ever played together on the same team. One night, while Joel and I were resting on the bench, our dad took a shot to the head. Some nut on the other team actually threw a punch at him!

Joel and I were over the boards before you could blink, the natural instincts of both hockey player and son making what happened next inescapable. Now this guy was big and in all honesty could have taken us individually, but three on one, he didn't have a chance. Let's just say it's a good thing the other players were there or who knows what we would have done—"bad things man, bad things."

After that incident, we became know as the Clark Boys and we were not to be messed with. The funny thing is, the Clark Boys aren't fighters. We are nice. Canadian, yes, but nice. But hockey is like that; sometimes it can turn nice Canadians into feisty Americans.

I am originally from Canada, eh. This pretty much guarantees two things. One, I'm funny but in an odd way, and two, I've loved and played the game of hockey since I took my first breath.

As a kid I ate, drank, and slept hockey. During hockey season, I would often have very early games. I would wake up for a game well before the alarm and shoot out of bed ready to play. I would check and double-check to make sure my gear was all accounted for, my stick was taped, and everything was ready. My dad would have to assure me that we were on time and that he knew where we were going, that my skates were sharp, and so on. I obsessed about being late. I didn't want to miss a moment.

When I was eighteen and graduating high school, I received the coveted invitation to tryouts. By then, I knew in my heart that I wasn't skilled enough to make a farm team, let alone the NHL. I was also beginning to have different aspirations, which entailed melody and rhythm. But it took getting cut in the third round to send me on another path. And just like that, my hockey career was over. It wasn't but a few years later that I started having strange dreams.

The dream started many different ways, but it had one theme and always ended the same. My dad and I would be on our way to my hockey game. Sometimes in the dream I was a teenager, other times I was much younger. Regardless, there was always a hockey game and I was always late. Often something would happen on the way to the rink, like a flat tire or traffic jam, and we would arrive just as the game was ending. The stress was very real.

In another scenario we would get to the ice rink on time and I would begin to gear up only to find that I had forgotten my laces, or my skates, or my stick, and I would have to watch the game from the bench while I waited for my dad to go get my gear. Then sometimes, for no reason whatsoever, the coach simply wouldn't put me in the game. And sometimes I would finally step out onto the ice just as it started melting and the ref would be forced to call the game. Whatever the scenario, there was one constant in every dream—I never got to play.

I would wake up angry. The frustration of not getting to play would stick with me all day. Sometimes before going to sleep, I would determine that this time I would actually play. I would visualize it as I fell asleep, but it never happened. The dream always played the same.

I had some version of this dream every five or six months over the course of ten years. The significance of these dreams did not occur to me until they went away.

My biggest fear in life? That I won't get to play—that I will never be ready, or good enough. I'm scared that all the games will be played, all the songs written, that Jesus will come back or take me home before I see the fullness of my promise. I'm being serious.

I would guess I am not alone in these feelings.

American Idol

I'm walking, waiting for You . . .

I was watching *American Idol* awhile back. For obvious reasons, my favorite part of the show is the beginning of each season. I imagine that's like watching someone jump out of

41

an airplane without a parachute. You don't want to see them bounce, but you just can't look away. So many of the contestants are desperate to be known; sadly most of them can't sing and apparently have tone deafness or dishonest friends or both.

But this one particular story took my breath away. A twenty-eight-year-old woman, at the top of the *American Idol* age limit that year, was married and had a little girl. She pawned off her wedding ring for just enough money to get to D.C. for the auditions. Her husband wasn't totally on board, but he was with her, and she was crying into the camera because if she didn't make the cut, she didn't know where they were going to sleep that night, as they were out of money.

Thankfully she could sing, and the judges, Simon included, passed her. When she came out, with tears in her eyes, she made a profound statement to this effect: "Finally some validation. It doesn't matter if I win, I *can* sing." It seemed she had waited most of her life to hear from an accredited source the words "You can sing. You are someone."

It's almost as if for a moment, the judges set her heart free from the haunting ghost, that ever-growing shadow of doubt regarding her ability to sing. For her, the audition wasn't just about winning a competition; it was about her promise. I think that's why she was crying—someone with "credentials" had recognized and therefore confirmed a part of her promise, her identity.

A couple of days later I was sitting at lunch with an older "professional" music minister, waiting for him to stop "preaching" at me, as if he had found all the most profound worship truths in the universe and apparently thought I didn't know the first thing about them. Yes, I was a little bugged.

"Listen," I wanted to say, "that's great stuff you got there, but I just wanted to hang out and eat a sandwich. I didn't sign up for the lecture."

So I got home from this meeting and I started complaining to Karen. "This guy just doesn't see the value in me. He treated me like I had just learned the earth wasn't flat. Can't he see that, just like him, I have a musical gifting and ability? Can't he recognize the promise God has given me? All we did was talk about him and what he knows! I know things too!" If it sounds like I was whining, it's because I was. If it sounds like I was searching for validation, it's because I was.

Karen reminded me, "Babe, you know what God has promised you, this guy doesn't have to see it for it to be true." I said, "I know, I know," but Karen just doesn't get it because apparently, I did need him to see it.

I'm convinced that one of the battles we face as believers is the one that rages between "being" and "being known." I believe God has placed a deep-seated need in our hearts. We long to be known, to have our promise validated by "an accredited source." This is a holy longing that only God can satisfy. He is the only true accredited source, the only one who can scratch the itch. Our validation is found in relationship with Him alone, and He loves us so much He will take us wherever we need to go to own this revelation.

Stupid Smelly Sheep

And if it's asked of me
To wait indefinitely
Then make my heart believe

I grew up in the church and therefore naturally developed a romantic view of the shepherd's life, as well as a fondness for sheep. You know, the children's storybook version, green rolling hills, 68 degrees, slight breeze, soft fluffy sheep, and camping all the time—which means a campfire with roasted hot dogs and S'mores. On top of that, shepherds had adventures. For instance, David had the bear and the lion; and when Jesus was born, the angels sang to the shepherds who "watched their flocks by night." Jesus also talked of how much He loved the sheep, so you can understand—to me the shepherd's life was just short of perfect.

However, as I've grown, so has my perspective. I no longer want to live at a McDonald's, be an astronaut, or play professional hockey (most of the time). The shepherd's life has lost its appeal too. It's hard work. There's rain, hours of boredom, and hundreds of smelly sheep—stupid, smelly sheep. No offense to you sheep enthusiasts, but in my opinion, only the cow is worse when it comes to intelligence . . . or maybe our puppy. Did I mention that we now have a puppy?

Samuel was famous in Israel; to meet him would have been equivalent today to meeting the Pope, only with less security. Not impressed? OK, how about this. It would be like meeting Bono. This is the guy who ran things before the people of Israel demanded a king—the man who anointed Saul that king. He heard from God on behalf of a nation. So when Samuel came, went through all the brothers, and brought David out from the field and anointed him, it was no little thing. It was a big deal. And then "the Spirit of GOD entered David like a rush of wind."[1]

I think that when the promise became publically recognized, it was oddly familiar to David. I can't imagine he'd ever dreamed he would be king. But I believe he recognized the promise when he heard it. He had been carrying and nurturing the seed in his heart for years. Then suddenly he is introduced to his promise. He is validated by an "accredited source." And I bet that once it was spoken, everything made sense, and then . . .

And then David goes back to tending sheep.

Have you ever experienced a time with God that was so profound, so holy, where for just a moment, everything was clear and your journey made sense?

Maybe it was when you were on your face in prayer, God was in the room, you felt the divine presence, and it was amazing. He spoke over you. He affirmed His promise and

His love to you. Maybe it was while listening to a song, reading a book, or watching a movie.

In that moment everything in the world fits together. Your past, present, and future are clear, your promise is rooted in your heart. You know you are loved, you know who you are, and you make the decision to believe it. And then . . .

And then Monday morning comes and you go back to that job. Or maybe you lose that job.

Or there is a family issue or an accident or even a death.

Or your company fails, your marriage crashes, your health slips away. . . .

And suddenly the promise seems no more than a distant memory, something beyond reality, too large to attain. Something tells me that for David, in one sense, tending sheep was easier, because now he knew the promise and it had been publicly recognized. But it also had to be tough, because even though the promise had been recognized, he was still "herding sheep."

I've been there—most of my life. And I think you know what I'm talking about. We all have a promise, but it often seems that after God confirms it, we go right back to tending sheep. I would like to suggest that how we choose to believe God during the "tending" makes a difference. Maybe all the difference.

Fringe

> *And if Your hand delays*
> *On godly plans well made*
> *Then give me eyes to see*

Shelved is a music industry term. Record labels will generally sign a band or individual for a span of two to six years. They sign them with the intention of making and selling albums for a profit. But if for whatever reason it looks like

45

the band won't make them money, they will "shelve" them, meaning that the band and their album will never see the light of day, as their album will not be released to stores. Trust me, it's a horrible experience if you're in the band.

As soon as I finished Bible college, I did what everyone expected. I started a band. OK, maybe not what *everyone* expected . . . I believe there is such a thing as the perfect song, a song so beautiful that to hear it would melt the hardest heart. A song so rock'n'roll that a body is inspired and must move. A song so true that God and all of heaven join in the singing. I am convinced that the perfect song could heal a broken world. I have not written it yet, but I've got time. Music is in me—I was created for melody. So if you truly knew me, the band wouldn't have surprised you.

I felt I had heard from God—He had given me words and Scriptures that encouraged me to believe that I was meant to make music for Him, and I believed that Fringe, the name of our band, was the means to that end. I am a singer and a songwriter, and for seven years I ate, slept, and breathed my band. At the time, I was positive that Fringe was the full expression of my promise.

For months, every other night of the week, we would practice until we finally felt we were good enough to play a show. We made a four-track recording and canvassed every bar and nightclub within a hundred miles. Then we went to open mic nights and battle of the bands until we began to line up gigs. More practice for the live album, our first! Then back to the street to line up more gigs . . . more practice, and countless hours writing songs. We played pretty much anywhere that would let us in the door. It didn't matter whether there were 10 people or 200; we played with everything we had. And the years passed.

Then we made our first studio record—a tribute to every independent band out there. We shopped it to every label under the sun. The Kinko's staff knew us by name—we practically lived there since that was the best place to put together press kits. We made hundreds. Then mail-out after mail-out, every record label got one. And then rejection letter after rejection letter until the day all bands covet, the phone call from a label. We were signed! More practice, more shows, and new band mates. More years pass by.

Finally the big payoff! We signed a six-year deal with another label—this label had money and connections! More practice and new songs for the new big-budget album with Grammy award–winning engineers and producers. Months in the studio, oh the beautiful process of recording an album with a real budget. Then mixing, photo shoots, magazine interviews, and bigger, better shows. Then the radio interviews as the single was released. The CD was packaged and sent out to magazines for reviews. The reviews started to come in—

"Trailing flashes of brilliance, traces of Matthews and U2's influence, but mostly just great and greatly produced songs of humble strength and unique sound. Fringe paints in the colors of wonder. This group is on top of the pile."[2]

And

"Clark's vocals have a richness, a fullness, surrounded with a harmony that borders on symphonic."[3]

And

"The lyrics are poetic, understated and intimately delivered. The band offers hope for the broken . . . imagine worship without the cliché, just the honesty."[4]

We had done it! All the hard work had finally paid off. Thank You, God! I was finally getting to live my promise! And then . . .

And then we heard the news. The label had lost their distribution. The album wasn't going to be released. The album was "shelved," but the label, due to their investment, decided to pick up the option in our contract. This meant we were contractually obligated to the label and couldn't make an-

47

other album for four years. And since the income from album sales (most of it from live shows) are a band's lifeblood. . . .

It was over.

And that's the story of my band.

Wilderness

I'm walking, waiting for You . . .

We were "shelved"—it was over and I couldn't believe it. My whole adult life had been given to the band. All those hockey dreams of me never getting to play came crashing home. I was miserable. It felt like I had been dragged into the wilderness, that place of disappointment, sorrow, and pain, where time itself seems to have forgotten you.

The next several years I lived in a spiritual wasteland much like the famed wilderness in the Bible where the Israelites spent forty years just hanging out. God was there with manna and water but not much else.

Before this season, I used to dread the idea of the wilderness; it was something to be avoided at all costs. But over the course of several years, I came to understand that if we breathe, we will experience wilderness seasons in life. Whether it's the loss of a loved one, a career derailed, or just a season of waiting, it's usually something we have little to no control over. What's crazy is that the wilderness season often comes right on the heels of receiving the promise.

I think many of us have experienced this phenomenon. We receive God's promise and then get "shelved." It's nothing new. If you look at the heroes in the Bible, most of them spent years on the shelf. Joseph, Moses, David—they all spent time "herding sheep" after the promise of God had been established in their hearts. They all did time in the wilderness.

In fact, Jesus Himself modeled this for us. After His baptism, He comes out of the water to a voice that shakes the heavens: "This is my beloved Son, with whom I am well pleased."[5] A dove descends and the Spirit of God rests on Him. Jesus's promise is made public.

At this point I would have expected Him to step out of the water and begin His signs and wonders, find men to disciple and miracles to do. Instead, Jesus steps out of the water, follows the Holy Spirit into the wilderness, and models for us what it's like to embrace your promise.

What is most amazing about this story is that it was God who led Jesus into the wilderness. The Bible tells us Jesus did nothing apart from His heavenly Father. He lived out the perfect will of God; Jesus willingly went into the wilderness.

I spent the first part of my life learning about my unique promise and the most recent part learning how to surrender it. I'm learning that the extent to which I possess my promise is directly linked to the measure of my surrender. Strangely, to truly participate in my promise now, I need to surrender it, and that's where the wilderness comes into play.

It's the wilderness that prepares our hearts. In the wilderness we learn to surrender our understanding of the promise. And in this surrender, we begin to see our promise through God's eyes. This is absolutely essential if we want to fully embrace our promise.

I now believe that the wilderness is the place where our relationship with God can be developed. This is a place where He can daily meet with us and provide for our needs. Where He can stretch and increase our capacity to believe with Him. Even in the midst of disappointment, sorrow, or pain, the wilderness can become a place of trust, beauty, and surrender. A place where we can meet God face-to-face and know His love, His grace, His kindness, and His goodness. It's one of the places where God can deepen our revelation of who He is in connection to where He wants to take us.

I wonder: if we were to go straight to the promise without the wilderness, would we believe enough to embrace the promise?

That being said, we must remember the wilderness is not our home. It is not our promise. It is not the end of the story. I know from experience that if believing wanes in the wilderness, you begin to settle there, thinking, *This must be as good as it gets.*

I'm afraid many Christians in wilderness seasons have stopped believing and taken up permanent residence, mistaking the wilderness for the Promised Land. There is nothing wrong with wilderness living as long as we understand it is not our home. There is so much more; we cannot settle there.

Bathtubs or Oceans

> *I stood on the edge to see what I could see*
> *Told my heart to never forget Your Spirit*
> *birthed in me*

When Eva was two, we went on a beach vacation. Weeks before the trip, the whole family told her about the ocean. "It's the biggest swimming pool ever!" Maddy informed her. "The waves are awesome!" Ethan explained. The entire drive to the coast, we regaled her with tales of the ocean. She was primed for big water.

After checking into the twenty-five-story beachfront condo, we immediately went out onto our balcony eighteen stories up to finally show Eva the unending body of water. Her eyes took it in and she finally understood. The ocean is big.

If you have been on a beach vacation with small kids, then you know it can easily take an hour from the moment you decide to go swimming to the moment you actually leave the condo. Especially if you have the Anglo-Saxon skin. The process seems endless: putting on bathing suits, gathering boogie boards, collecting towels, selecting beach toys, packing the cooler, and lathering on sunscreen in generous amounts upon every surface that could even possibly see a moment of sun.

Along the way, the kids become almost unbearable. Their understanding of "be patient" is waiting three minutes between asking, "When are we going to the beach?"

While we prepared, Eva got caught up in her older brother and sister's euphoric expectation. The kids would run to the balcony and look at the "osen," as Eva called it, and laugh. Then Ethan would exclaim that he was going to ride the biggest wave. Then they would come find us to ask, "Aren't we ready yet?" and "Can we go now?"

Finally, everyone lathered in sunscreen, towels accounted for, flip-flops on, we headed for the door. I did a head count, Eva was not among us. I called for her. "Eva, let's go swim in the osen! Eva?" There was no response. I walked through the condo and finally found her naked in the master bathroom trying to get into the tub. "What are you doing?" I asked.

"Mmm take a baff, Daddy," she said.

"What about the ocean?"

My daughter, upon seeing the bathtub, forgot about the ocean. She was more than willing to trade the ocean she had not experienced for the familiarity of the tub.

Suddenly God spoke to my heart and said, "Jason, the promises I have for you are the size of the ocean. Don't get distracted by bathtubs."

The moral?

Not all water is created equal. Your promise, my promise—it's huge! It's as big as the ocean. We can't afford to lose sight of it or we will be tempted to settle for bathtubs.

Embracing Our Promise

> *There is a freedom found in surrender*
> *My sacrifice, my song to You*

In Matthew 5:14, Jesus says, "If I make you light-bearers, you don't think I'm going to hide you under a bucket, do you?

I'm putting you on a light stand" (Message). I'm convinced God wants to show us off for the whole world to see. He wants to show us off for His glory. But when the recognition comes, it will be a by-product of God's recognition.

Jesus did nothing apart from His Father. He waited until He was thirty before being released into His public ministry. He surrendered himself to the wilderness and later the cross. He was always patient, never forcing the Holy Spirit. He perfectly walked out the fulfillment of His promise, and everything He did glorified His father. He had no agenda higher than that, and He fully embraced His promise from His first breath to His ascension.

An insecurity haunts humankind, a holy insecurity or void, and only God can fill it. I cannot allow my worth to be determined by the eyes of "accredited sources." My promise is not defined by the applause of peers. My promise is embraced through surrender. It's found through the obscurity of a wilderness where my focus shifts from me to Him.

Whether we are called to Hollywood or Haiti, it's our surrender that defines us. It is God's intention that we all get to play. God is the one who created the game and gave us the passion and ability. I believe he is teaching us how to live bigger. And to live bigger we have to be intimate with surrender. Embracing the promise is about surrendering it back to Him and allowing Him to define it and fulfill it in His timing and not forcing ours. It's showing patience, standing firm, and believing in the face of devastating heartache and incredible obstacles. Embracing the promise could look like waiting, even death. But embracing the promise is the only way to truly be alive.

4

The Believe Switch

The Audible Voice

Made good on grace, surrendered to the winds
Up and away, the life I was born to live

Note: I have changed the names in the following story because it's funnier . . . and because my sister told me too.

Have you ever heard the audible voice of God, the actual, audible voice? On a daily basis I encounter God through reading, or prayer, and of course music. Throughout the day, He speaks to me. And then there have been the profound, unmistakable meetings with God where I've experienced the power of His presence in my heart, mind, body, and soul.

But there was one time I heard Him speak audibly. It's only happened once and this is what He said: "You're kissing another man's wife."

When I was ten years old, the kids in my class started to tease me about Wonder Woman (name changed). There was a song they loved to sing when Wonder Woman and I were in the same room. It went like this: "Jason and Wonder Woman sitting in a tree / K-I-S-S-I-N-G / First comes love, then comes marriage / then comes a baby in the baby carriage." It's a catchy tune; it gets in your head.

The song really didn't bother me much; I was only slightly embarrassed. But more than anything, I was surprised. In all honesty, at that point in my life I hadn't even thought about the love part yet. And why were we in a tree?

But the kids kept singing the song and Wonder Woman seemed nice, so I started considering it. Ten children seemed about right, I even came up with a few names—Talon, Blade, and Lightning . . . and then of course Thunder. And as far as the kissing was concerned, did we really have to?

One night my dad overheard my sister, Aimee, and I talking about the impending nuptials. He called me over. "Jason, you are too young to be thinking about girls." And that was that, the wedding was called off and I stopped thinking about Wonder Woman and our ten kids. When I was young, many things were just easier. If Dad said, "Don't worry about it," well, then I stopped worrying about it.

However, three years later I met Princess Leia (again, name changed). She was my sister's best friend. I liked her and I didn't need anyone singing songs about baby carriages to be convinced. She was pretty and nice and, well, I don't think my dad could have talked me out of this one. I was smitten.

For months, Aimee, Princess Leia, my friend Fonzie (yeah, Fonzie—what the heck?), and I would hang out. Our favorite place was the mall, and between the mall and youth group, Leia and I developed a friendship that would make you giggle.

Then one night our youth group had a big cookout at a farm that belonged to a church member. It was one of those magical nights with a bonfire, a hayride, caramel apples, and of course, the princess. Leia smelled nice and she laughed at my jokes and at one point we began to hold hands. It was absolutely amazing.

Late in the evening, we all went for a walk. Somewhere along the way, Aimee and Fonzie lagged behind, and suddenly I was alone with Leia. I could hear the Tiffany song in my head, "I think we're alone now, there doesn't seem to be any one a-rah-hound . . ." I was holding her hand and I could barely breathe. Before I could think of anything to say or do, she kissed my cheek, then turned and ran back to the bonfire, laughing.

About four months later my family moved to the Northwest and Princess Leia's family moved to Indiana. But Leia and Aimee stayed in touch, and over the years the princess and I would write each other and occasionally talk on the phone. I never forgot that kiss, and so when she came out to visit us one summer, we picked up right where we left off. At the age of seventeen, Princess Leia officially became my girlfriend, and at the age of eighteen, I left home for a job.

This job allowed me to travel through Indiana on a regular basis. As Princess Leia lived with her parents, whenever I came through I would stay at her house and we would go out on a date. Love, true love. I wrote her a beautiful song about climbing mountains and swimming oceans just to see her. Imagine that Bryan Adams song from Kevin Costner's *Robin Hood* and you pretty much got it . . . It made her cry.

When I wasn't with her, I would spend hours writing her letters and dreaming about what life would be like with her in it. In fact, there were no future scenarios without her. In my mind we were married with kids, already pros at the K-I-S-S-I-N-G.

One night while I was praying, I realized that I had given an awful lot of my heart to Princess Leia and hadn't even considered asking God about it. I began to converse with God, and as I did, He pointed out that I had gone pretty far down the road of my future without including Him in any of the decisions. Then God asked me if He or Princess Leia was first in my life. When I realized that I couldn't answer this question correctly, I became depressed and frustrated.

Over the next month I agonized in my prayer life as God kept gently bringing this question back to my heart. Finally I said, "OK, God, I want to put You first, but I really like Princess Leia. What's a man to do?"

I felt like God asked me to take a break. I was frustrated and yet I trusted God and His love. And so in my heart I determined that the next time I saw Leia, I would obey God and put our relationship on hold. The next time I saw her ended up being the following week.

I arrived in the afternoon and spent a few hours with her family before taking her out on a dinner date. I planned on breaking the news over dinner, but the way she looked at me got me worrying about her feelings. But I knew she loved God and I felt that she would not only understand but would also probably be quite impressed with my godliness. Still, I decided to wait and tell her after dinner. Maybe in the car, I thought.

After dinner we drove around until eventually we found a church parking lot. It was a true country church—in the middle of a field in the middle of nowhere. I planned on telling her during the drive, but she was holding my hand. When we parked, I turned on the tape deck—U2's "I Still Haven't Found What I'm Looking For." I rolled down the windows and we took a blanket and sat on the hood of the car. "OK, God, I'll tell her now," I thought. Then I kissed her.

And then I heard it. I kid you not. In an audible voice, God said, "You are kissing another man's wife!"

It was so loud and so strong that I jerked back from Princess Leia. I looked at her to see if she had heard it, but she simply looked confused; apparently she hadn't heard anything. But I had. I was so shaken up, not just by my failure but also by the message. Princess Leia wasn't mine. Bono cooed, "I still haven't found what I'm looking for . . ."

Princess Leia married a nice fella a year or two later.

That seems long ago now, in a galaxy far away. You know, God's plans for our lives are so much grander than ours. His thoughts always surpass ours. His dreams are bigger and better than we could ask or imagine. His goodness is beyond our comprehension. I learned this firsthand a year later when, at Bible college, I met my wife-to-be, my Karen. No one is more perfect than she is. And God knew this! He saw my future and said, "It is good!" On top of all of that, I *get* to kiss her! We have three perfect kids with really cool names, and that's better than any man could hope for. As Bono says, "Even better than the real thing."

So God has a plan. He is never caught off guard or surprised, and if we say *yes* to Him, if we are willing to trust and obey He will work it in us. I have learned that He doesn't always tell us *why*. He rarely gives us the whole picture or interpretation, He rarely speaks out loud, but He will guide us—He can be trusted.

I have also come to see that God has perfect timing. We can push our own agendas or we can rest and chase after Him. In my prayer time, God was gently telling me He had something else—something better for me. However, I was so blinded by my idea of what it should look like that I wasn't able to see.

I have grand promises from God, yet oddly enough, I have had a hard time along the way trusting Him to bring them to fruition. I've often gotten an idea and found myself mid-chase before discussing it with God. I have tracked things down and made things happen. I can almost always make it work. I can almost always make something fit. But thankfully God in His mercy and grace has stepped in every time and said, "Jason, this isn't My best for you" or "No, this isn't My plan, it's yours." Then there was the time he said, "Hey, you are kissing another man's wife!"

Sometimes I think I know the best ending to my story even though at the age of five I asked God to be the author. But I am learning that even when God leads me to a place that seems contrary to everything I understand, in the end, I know that His characters always get the girl (figuratively). The question is not *will God let me down?* but *will I surrender?* Will I trust and obey?

Giving It Back

> *I've said You're the Son of God and I've forced water from a stone*
> *And I've searched my heart's ruins till Your heart was found*

I was standing near the back of the concert hall at a Delirious show, watching the band lead a few thousand people into a rock 'n' roll worship experience. It was about eight months since my band Fringe had ceased to exist. I was miserable. There I was watching a group of guys do what I was promised. It felt like they were living my promise. They were up there doing what I was created to do. I felt like God had discarded me. The word *fringe* took on a whole new meaning.

Karen and I left early. On the drive home she started talking about the concert, about the kids, about life in general. After a short time she realized I was so emotionally exhausted that if I opened my mouth, I would no doubt fall apart. She sensed my pain, she took my hand in hers, and we drove the rest of the way home in silence. When we walked in the door, I didn't even acknowledge the babysitter. I walked past her to our bedroom and into the bathroom. That's as far as I got. I collapsed onto the bathroom floor.

I remember lying there, crying out to God my absolute sadness, as the ghost of my promise tortured me with my failures. For so long I had been haunted by my promise of music. But that dream was over, that night the music died and I just couldn't understand it. I remember telling God that it felt as if He had made me into a hammer and then kept asking me to cut something. (I often think in analogies and this was the best analogy I could come up with for what I was feeling.) Why give me a promise if there was no intention of fulfilling it?

I had spent seven years keeping the dream alive, kicking and scratching and clawing and pulling and working and sweating and grinding out a future in music because that's where my promise was. That's what you have to do, right? In the end, I had failed and I was utterly heartbroken and exhausted.

That night I had a decision to make. I didn't know I had a decision at the time, but by the grace of God I made the right one. That night, after hours of crying out to God, I found myself at the difficult and beautiful place known as the cross. That night I surrendered my promise back to God.

Though I didn't see the fullness of it at the time, looking back, that was the moment I began living my promise, that is the moment I fully embraced it. That was the moment I made a shift from unbelief to believing. The next morning with absolutely no agendas, I went up to my music room and wrote a song. Some of the lyrics go like this:

> Come let's go, up to the mountain. Come let's
>   worship beneath the Cross.
> Come let's know our Savior's journey and find
>   our story in His song . . .

Once you experience a revelation in your heart, it takes some time to walk it out. That is to say, my heart was changed but my life did not immediately reflect that change. I had to begin to make the transition in my thinking and in my actions. The next few years were what I refer to as a season of the renewing of my mind.[1] God began changing the way I think and that began to affect everything. Everything practical, emotional, and spiritual began to be viewed through the heart of God and His love. I made a decision to lay everything down, and in so doing I made a decision to believe.

The Believe Switch

> Faith is not the absence of doubt: it's the presence of belief. I may not always feel that I have great faith. But I can always obey.
>
> Bill Johnson, *When Heaven Invades Earth*

Just because you make the decision to believe doesn't mean life suddenly hands you unicorns and rainbows. So, how does one believe? I mean, there isn't a believe switch. You either do or you don't.

I struggled with day-to-day belief. I was shocked by my cynicism and by how much unbelief I had lived with. This ugly thing known as realism seemed to be how I approached almost every aspect of life. Somehow, I had become a saved unbeliever, and I was determined to change that. I had only one prayer throughout this season: "God, help me believe."

One Mississippi summer day, after working eight hours on a roof in the 98 degree heat, I asked God with sweaty sincerity, "Do You have a believe switch? If You've got one, I would sure like to know what it looks like and where to find it." He responded to my heart by saying, "I've got one, it's called obedience. Your surrender to My good and perfect will. You're doing great! I love you and I'm proud of you!"

And so I began a journey. An intentional step-by-step surrender to the good and perfect will of God. I chose to chase obedience, and in so doing, I chose to trust. As the days turned to months, I began to notice that the ghost of my promise wasn't haunting me as strongly as it always had. I began to realize that even though my circumstances didn't appear to be relevant to my promise, I was able to believe.

60

Here is what I am learning. Obedience births believing, and what's amazing is that, if you practice obedience enough, believing becomes part of who you are.

I really do think this is what Paul was talking about when he wrote about the renewed mind. The Scripture says, "Do not conform any longer to the pattern of this world, but be transformed by the renewing of your mind. Then you will be able to test and approve what God's will is—his good, pleasing and perfect will."[2] The mind is renewed through a believing heart and the believing heart is birthed through surrendered obedience.

I want a renewed mind, because with it I can hear the heartbeat of God. With a renewed mind I can know all God wants and His wants can become mine. I am convinced that's how to truly embrace our promise.

Obedience

I came believing with righteous intent
To lay hold of innocence

For the longest time I had a hard time explaining to my satisfaction why I disciplined my kids. Is it so they can be respectable contributing members of society, or is it so they can understand the value of rules? I guess, maybe, uhhh, no, that's not it . . . Is it so they can be well rounded, civilized, or nice? I hope not.

I've always made my love known while disciplining my kids. And rarely am I upset—well, there was that time I lost it because my two-year-old thought poop made for good art. Karen and I are still not quite sure what he was drawing on his bedroom wall, but I'd put my money on a spaceship. "You don't play with your poop," I kept saying, until Karen asked me to leave. Really I was just shocked that it was something that had to be taught . . .

Sorry, I'm back.

So when I discipline my kids, there is always the explanation of "You have to learn how to obey." But why is that so important?

In Acts, Paul and his entourage are out preaching the gospel, and one day Paul says, "I feel compelled by the Holy Spirit to go back to Jerusalem. I'm not sure what is going to happen, but I'm pretty sure it won't be easy. In fact, the Holy Spirit has made it clear that there are hard times ahead" (paraphrase).[3] When those around Paul heard this, they begged him not to go, yet from town to town Paul ignores their pleas and continues on. When he reaches the town of Ptolemais, a prophet from another town meets him. This prophet had come with a word from the Holy Spirit. He walks up to Paul and with great showmanship tells Paul that if he continues on to Jerusalem, he will be tied hand and foot. More or less, Paul was bound for a jail cell or worse.

It's not that the prophet and those around Paul hadn't heard God. But they interpreted God's message incorrectly. God had asked Paul to go to Jerusalem. So the issue wasn't whether he should go, it's how do they believe with him on the journey? How do they trust God with him?

This is what Paul had to say about it. "Why do you insist on making a scene and making it even harder on me? You're looking at this backward. The issue in Jerusalem is not what they do to me, whether arrest or murder, but what the Master Jesus does through my obedience."[4]

It is because I love my kids that I must teach them about the importance of obedience. I believe God has amazing things He wants my kids to do with Him, and the better understanding they have about obedience, the bigger God can use them. Obedience is the response of a heart that knows love. Obedience is surrender; it's the doorway to fulfillment and the key to living wild. It's this kind of obedience that defines world changers.

Oswald Chambers put it this way: "The promises of God are of no value to us until, through obedience, we come to understand the nature of God."[5] It is in obedience that we grow in His love and it is in obedience that He finds us trustworthy with the deeper longings of His heart. Obedience is what lands us in the best stories, the ones where we get to experience overwhelming circumstances and then we get to discover His wonderful faithfulness.

Obedience is an amazing thing; the more we obey, the more opportunities God has to reveal Himself. It's the greater revelation of God's heart that releases us to fully embrace our promise.

Past Comfortable

> *I believe it's begun and is finished, a revolution*
> *of the cross*
> *I've awakened to a movement, love my bur-*
> *den, the birthplace of holiness*

When it comes to embracing our promise, our biggest enemy is comfort.

Don't get me wrong, when it's time to sleep, I want my king-size bed and my beautiful Karen to scratch my head. And I must have a fan—not because I'm hot, but for the noise. I can't have wind blowing on me because it dries out my throat. The sheets have to be at least 400 thread count and . . . well, you get the point. I like comfort . . . and . . . I'm a princess.

While it's perfectly fine to enjoy the wonders of down comforters, we will not fully embrace our promise unless we're willing to step beyond comfortable.

God will often invite us into uncomfortable situations in order to reveal His love. He will ask for crazy obedience in order to show He is trustworthy. He will say something like, "Come to Me" while He is standing on water in the middle of a raging storm. But here is the thing—if we trust and obey, we get to walk on water!

What I've begun to realize is that, though I want to see God move miraculously, I rarely allow myself to be in a situation where I need a miracle. So I have recently decided that I can't live comfortably. There must always be something in my life I'm believing for, something that's bigger than me, bigger than my abilities and resources. There must always be a place in my life where I need a miracle, a place of full surrender and total dependence.

I'm a novice when it comes to living in the miraculous, but I don't want to remain so. I am hungry for God's presence, so I'm simply saying *yes*, *yes* to obedience and *yes* to advancing the kingdom.

5

Do It for the Story

Crazy

> *I saw the burning bush*
> *I went to take a look*
> *You were there*

I come from a family of storytellers. When we all get together, as you might assume, we tell stories. We love to laugh and reminisce . . . *oh, man, do you remember when?* We love the mischievous memories and the daring-dangerous tales. We love to hear about what God is doing in the lives of those in the room, of the *you've got to be kidding!* and the *wow, doesn't God love us!* Our absolute, hands-down favorites are the wild God stories.

I was sitting at a table outside of Starbucks in an outdoor shopping plaza. I was writing there and planned on meeting

Karen and the kids a little later for some shopping. I was enjoying a caramel macchiato when Westerfield walked by.

"Hey, man!" I waved.

Westerfield is unlike anyone I've met before. He's crazy and he believes in miracles. I'm not saying those two things always go together, but they do with Westerfield. When I first met him, I believed in miracles too, but more in theory. Not Westerfield—he travels around the world and he has seen God heal blindness and deafness and so much more. I am not kidding.

One evening earlier that week I had gone with Westerfield into Charlotte on what he called a "treasure hunt." We were looking for people to pray for. And when we found them, Westerfield went crazy. I mean, he cut straight to the heart of how much God loved the person we were talking to. If it sounds uncomfortable, that's because it was.

It was also beautiful. I stood with Westerfield at a bus stop while he shared with a fella about the personal love of God. Westerfield was able to reveal to this guy the love of God for his life—past, present, and for the days ahead. While talking with the guy, Westerfield suddenly asked if he could pray for his girlfriend and sick baby.

The guy's eyes got wide. "How could you know that?" he asked.

"That's how much God loves you, He put your family on my heart," Westerfield said, and then he prayed, asking God to release His love on this guy and his family. And God did. The guy stood there in the street and cried as he experienced God's loving-kindness through Westerfield. And when it was over, not only was this guy blessed, heaven had a new citizen!

"Hey man! Hold on," Westerfield said as he walked by my Starbucks table. Then he turned and chased down an eighteen-year-old fella out shopping with what appeared to be his girlfriend. I got up and followed him. He introduced himself and then, just like that, started telling the guy about

God's love. I stood uncomfortably beside him. These kids were cool, they did most of their shopping at the Buckle and obviously had somewhere to go, I thought to myself. However, even though Westerfield was being crazy again, and seemed to be breaking all the unspoken social rules for interacting with strangers, it was OK because of what I had witnessed with him earlier in the week.

Westerfield may be crazy and uncomfortable to hang out with in public, but he carries such a revelation of the love of God that I'm more than willing to be uncomfortable and even a little crazy. Plus Westerfield has some amazing God stories. And I want my own God stories.

After he shared the goodness of God with this young couple, we headed back to my table and began to talk. It didn't take long until Westerfield wanted to pray. *Right here?* I thought, uncomfortable again. OK.

It was amazing. Seriously. I felt God come alive in me. I imagine it was something like an Upper Room experience. I had such a revelation of God's love that I had to worship and it had to be out loud. Both Westerfield and I began to praise God right there at Starbucks, breaking more rules for socially accepted behavior.

I am a fairly reserved person. I have only danced in public twice in my life. Once on my first date with Karen—I felt it was a necessary sacrifice to get the girl. And once at my sister Aimee's wedding, out of respect for the holiness of her day. So praising God out loud at a Starbucks is, well, not like me. People walked by and looked at us oddly. We probably looked like idiots. But I didn't care.

You know David, my favorite Old Testament character; he worshiped God by dancing in front of a nation in his underwear.[1] So really, this outburst of praise at Starbucks wasn't that big a deal. First, I didn't dance, and second, we kept our clothes on. Honestly, on this surrendered and untamed journey, I am learning that sometimes worship can look foolish.

Finally we hugged and went our separate ways. Karen, Maddy, and Ethan had joined us near the end, and Maddy had five dollars burning a hole in her pocket. So we went around the corner to a Pottery Barn for kids, or something like that. I was drunk with love for Jesus and was still worshiping Him and praying in my heart when we entered the store. I remember praying, "Lord, make me bolder, more courageous. God, give me cool stories. Let me see You at work as I walk through my day . . . even now."

One of the salesladies walked by and I felt like God said, "Go ask her if you can pray for her sick husband." I know that sounds crazy, but that's what I heard God say to my heart.

"Well . . . um . . . OK, God." I was suddenly uncomfortable again. I headed her way, a little nervous because of being a freshman at this sorta thing. The saleslady went into the back before I could get to her. "Employees Only," the sign said. I wasn't sure what I was supposed to do next. I wasn't positive I'd heard God right, but I didn't want to miss a chance for a good story.

Me—"God, tell ya what, if she comes back out with something in her left hand, spins twice, and her right shoe is untied, then I will go speak to her."

God—"How about if she just comes back out?"

Me—"OK."

She did. So I went up to her. "Excuse me, but are you married?"

"Yes," she said, confused.

"Is your husband sick?"

"Yes." Now *she* looked uncomfortable.

"Well, God loves you both so much that He told me about your husband and I believe He wants me to pray for him," I said in a rush.

Her eyes welled up with tears and she told me her story.

Her husband had recently gone to Chicago on a business trip and had become ill. He spent seven days in his hotel room until finally a friend had flown up to help take him to a hospital where he had spent the last few days.

I prayed for her husband and we traded email addresses. Later I received an email that her husband was home and well!

Do It for the Story

> *It's time to change the world,*
> *To live life true and wild,*
> *My revolution of the heart.*

When he was eighteen, my brother Joel told me he came up with a life theme or motto: "Do it for the story." At first, I thought Joel's theme was a little irresponsible. I mean, a life theme should be something more Mother Teresa-ish, like "Sacrifice for the poor, sick, and oppressed." Shouldn't it? But the more I thought about it, the more I liked Joel's life theme. I've thought about it even more over the years, and I've concluded it's simply brilliant! Yes, do it for the story.

I'm currently in hot pursuit of wild God stories myself. I have moved and stayed for them, literally and figuratively. I will go halfway around the world for them. I once shared with a group of believers in the Philippines that I had come in search of God stories—really, that's what I said.

How do we find wild God stories? One word: experience. I believe we were created for experience—to taste and touch, to search and discover. Why else does a thirteen-month-old experience such joy in the discovery of a light switch or bubbles? OK, I get bubbles. Why is it that I find joy at the top of a mountain? And why did God leave it to Adam to name the animals? God created them, it seems He would be the best suited to name them. Yet from the beginning, God set up the universe with all of its wonders and mysteries for our discovery, for our pleasure. Our relationship with God works the same way. We have been invited to discover Him and experience His heart until we begin to see, hear, and feel as He does . . . and we find ourselves doing it for the story, our story, His story.

Scary Is Fun

*I want to live this life in the brilliance of Your
   song
I want to worship You with a life fully sung
   . . . a beautiful song*

We were on vacation in the wild Northwest. Vancouver Island, to be specific. My daughter Maddy was almost three years old. We were at the deep end of the local public indoor pool and she was on the diving board. It was at least as far away from the water as she was tall, and she was tall for her age. It had been her idea to jump and had seemed like a good idea from the shallow end. I waited in the water right below the diving board encouraging her, but to no avail. It was "too high" and "too scary."

Earlier in the week I had gone cliff jumping, a good seventy-five feet of it. I love rivers and have an unwavering opinion that they were created for my enjoyment. So when I see a river, I generally want to get in it. How I get in it is where the fun begins.

Pete, a good friend from the area, and I had hiked out to the river and spent about an hour swimming at the bottom of its beautiful 75-foot waterfall. After we finished swimming, we began the climb back up the trail. The trail sawbacked the side of the falls and we arrived at the top just in time to watch dumbfounded as a guy jumped into the water below.

Both Pete and I have done some cliff jumping in our day, but when we first saw the falls, we hadn't even considered it—it was really high. But once I saw the guy's head pop out of the water, I realized it could be done without dying.

And so while Pete, with his back to me, talked to one of the jumper's friends at the cliff edge, I talked to myself.

"It's just two steps and you're over the edge." My eyes focused on the edge. "Just two steps." I took a deep breath. "Just two steps." I removed my shoes. "Just two steps." I took off my shirt. "Just two steps." I took another breath and then I took the two steps, and as I dropped, I sensed Pete turn and I heard him say, "Oh, Jason!"

It was an amazing experience and also a great story. One Pete and I have told and relived in the telling many times since. You see, Pete is not one to watch someone else get a good story without him. Within ten seconds, he had followed me over the edge. I still smile when picturing him eye rolling and muttering under his breath while quickly removing his shoes and shirt and then taking those two steps.

When we got back to the hotel, Maddy heard our stories. Now, it's hard to explain to a three-year-old why anyone would jump off a cliff. Three-year-olds don't have the capacity to understand this. The best I could do by way of explanation is "Sometimes, scary is fun."

So as I treaded water under the diving board, I reminded her again. "Honey, sometimes scary is fun!" She was a hard sell, but I persisted until we finally came to an agreement—I would jump with her. So I joined her on the diving board. "It's just two steps."

I would love to tell you that it wasn't too high, that her head didn't go under, and that there was nothing but joy in her eyes. But that would be a lie. The truth is, Maddy kept a death grip on me until we reached the side of the pool; she was convinced she had made a mistake. But once we got there, safe, she began to laugh with the wonder of the whole experience. I did too.

My little girl beat the diving board. Yes, it was too scary and too high, but she did it anyway. She jumped—for herself, for me, for the story. Years later, most of that vacation has faded from her memory, but the story of the diving board lives on. And "scary is fun" has become a household phrase.

Now let me give you a father's perspective. Before and after she jumped, I was enthusiastic in my encouragement. When we reached the side of the pool, I was immersed in her joy. For the rest of the week I was overwhelmed with pride. She had believed; she had lived fully and I got to be a part of it. I was her catalyst, her savior, and her friend. And together we beat the diving board. The wonder of my daughter's trust and then the opportunity to be faithful with it are a father's dream come true. If she had not jumped, we both would have missed out. But she did jump and now she owns that story. She owns that experience. And the diving board no longer controls her fear.

It's a great story.

God Is Not Safe

> God is not trying to keep you safe,
> He is trying to keep you from a meaningless life!
>
> Kris Vallotton, author of *Purity*

I remember leading worship one evening at a church we were attending. Afterward, the very friendly pastor said, "That was amazing." Then he said something that has kind of become a regular phrase between Karen and me when we think something is weird or crazy. He said, "You are two weeks and a tambourine ahead of us."

I now understand that he was not complimenting me but graciously dismissing me.

I spent three years with that church, and the message I heard time and again was that it was a safe place to come and fellowship. In fact, it seemed like that was the message I heard in most of the churches I visited. The problem was that I had already experienced the revolutionary who goes by the name *Jesus*. And there was nothing about Him that was safe. At least not the way I'd come to understand the word.

As time progressed, I realized the friendly pastor's comment was just a polite observation. This particular church was comfortable where it was. And I think that's how most of us define safety, by how comfortable we are.

When we boil a relationship with God down to how comfortable we are at any given moment, we step away from intimacy and into religious form. I once saw a bumper sticker that illustrates this well. I know it was created with good intentions, but it's always bothered me: "Take your kids to Sunday school this Sunday, they need and deserve it." The problem with this statement is that both my kids and I don't need Sunday school, we need Jesus. We may learn about Him in Sunday school, but the sticker's premise is wrong. If you want to lose a generation, raise them to know the names of God but never experience the interpretations—Loving, Intimate, Majestic, Holy, Consuming Fire . . .

Humankind is born for communion with God. Our hearts are designed for wild worship, yet we're often offered rote liturgy. Our minds are designed to dream as big as the heart of God, but we're immersed in the latest building plans. Our bodies are designed for dangerous service; we're taught biblical commentaries from the safety of a pew or a comfortable theatre chair.

Please hear my heart. I'm not condemning how we structure a Sunday morning service; I'm challenging why we meet. There is nothing wrong with liturgy; the Bible is filled with it. There's nothing wrong with building plans; I like to worship under a roof, especially when it's raining. And we need Scripture; it's absolutely essential. But at the end of the day, if we haven't touched the heart of God, if we haven't experienced His glory, if we haven't encountered His nature—evidence of one of His many names—then the gathering is irrelevant. I'm all for Sunday school if it drives us headlong into Jesus and His story. He must be experienced. And not just on Sunday.

The wild God stories are the ones full of "too high" and "too scary" but we jump anyway. They are the stories entered into through discomfort. They're really the only stories worth living.

Six Floors and an Escort

I will stay awhile, let my heart beat with Yours
I'm dancing to Your melody
And I can feel You, see You, know You, praise
  You
You're everything to me

Aimee is my sister, my only sister. She has always felt deeply; she loves big. Everything about her is authentic. She doesn't put on airs, and when she gives you a compliment, which she often does, it releases such life because there is no falseness in it.

My sister loves Joel's motto ("do it for the story") and recently she decided to get her own story.

Aimee was driving by a hospital near her home when she felt God tugging on her heart: "Go in there and love the people."

As she walked into the hospital, she asked God to lead her to someone who really needed a visit. There were six floors in the hospital; she figured she'd start on the first and work her way up to the sixth floor.

First Floor

Now, there are rules about this sort of thing. You can't just go walking through a hospital. Aimee wasn't interested in making waves; she wanted to be respectful of the nurses and their stations, so she made her way to the first-floor desk. There was a wall of glass between her and the nurse. Aimee, uncomfortable because she had never done this before, leaned in and asked the nurse if there was anyone who might be in need of a visit. "Maybe someone who doesn't have family around," she said.

The first floor nurse immediately teared up. Then she got really close to the glass and spoke softly, "There is a girl on this floor that really needs prayer. I can't tell you who it is or her room number, but she is in isolation."

Aimee, pleasantly surprised by the welcome, simply said, "Thanks," and went in search of the girl in isolation. She found her but couldn't get into her room. Aimee prayed in the hallway and then decided to head for the second floor.

She was just about to get into the elevator when the same nurse found her and said, "I just want to encourage you to continue on, listening to that still small voice." Then she hugged Aimee tightly and thanked her. Aimee didn't feel like she had done anything worthy of this affection, but feeling more confident, she headed to the second floor.

Second Floor

Aimee couldn't find a nurse so she decided to just walk down a hall. On her left, in a hospital bed, lay a woman watching *The Price is Right*. She walked in, introduced herself. The lady's name was Faye.

"Faye, I was driving by the hospital and felt like I was supposed to stop by and visit you," Aimee said. "Is there anything I can pray for?" Faye told her story—she was anemic and had passed out in Walmart and woke up at the hospital. Aimee asked if she could pray for Faye's condition. "I don't ever refuse prayer," Faye said. "Me neither," Aimee replied.

Third Floor

On the third floor, Aimee found a nurse at the station. She was getting better at this, and with a little more confidence she again asked if there was anyone she could visit with. This third floor nurse didn't tear up, she looked at Aimee suspiciously and said, "Everyone on the third floor is just fine." Aimee, uncomfortable again, quietly thanked her and headed for the fourth floor.

Fourth Floor

Another nurses station, another nurse. More tears.

"Really? You came here to visit someone? That's amazing. I have to find someone for you, surely there is someone, come with me, this is so sweet, you came to visit someone, so sweet . . ." The nurse hardly took a breath.

In the end, they couldn't find anyone. One lady was in surgery and another had family. They went back to the nurse's station and the nurse said, "I can't believe someone finally came and we have no one. I'm so sorry," she said through tears. She hugged Aimee like she was family and then Aim went to the elevator.

Fifth Floor

Riding up to the fifth floor, Aimee began to ponder on the two hugging nurses. They were so touched and she really didn't feel like she had done anything. "God, is that why I am here?" she wondered.

She stepped off the elevator and was met by the fifth-floor nurse. More tears, hugs, and help. She pointed her to the room of an eighty-seven-year-old woman. Her name was Margaret and she didn't look well. She was so small in the bed—fragile. She was confused when she met Aimee. But she warmed up quickly when Aimee told her she had come to hear her story.

"Sit down, dear," she said as she motioned to a chair. Margaret was hard of hearing and even harder to understand. She spoke softly. She had four children, her husband was still alive, they lived in Franklin, Tennessee, her whole life, and she was at the hospital because she'd almost had a heart attack.

Aimee told the story about her family, her two girls, and her husband, Eric. Then she prayed quietly in her heart for Margaret and Margaret's living husband and kids. Just before leaving, Aimee brushed Margaret's silver hair back off her face and told her she had the most beautiful eyes.

Aimee left Margaret in prayer. "God, I just want to love more, I want to have my own stories of Your love. I want to see Your miracles released through me . . . I want to practice giving freely what You have so generously given me—Your love." Aimee was there for love, for the story.

Sixth Floor

She got off the elevator and immediately noticed a big security guard looking at her. He seemed to have been waiting for her as well. He was a bit intimidating, she thought. As she started for the desk, he walked over to her and said, "Why are you here, miss?"

"I'm visiting people."

"Who are you visiting?" he asked.

"I'm just visiting anyone the nurses tell me I can—those who don't get many visitors."

Before Aimee had finished talking, another guard showed up. One guard was a little overwhelming, two guards . . . it was a little scary. *Is there a "visiting hospital patients jail"?* she wondered.

This guy was shorter and less kind. He started asking the same questions with one addition: "Who were you looking for on the third floor?" Apparently the third-floor nurse had called in the cavalry.

He took her ID and went to a phone. She was left with the first guard who was writing notes down in a little pad. Aimee noticed the sixth-floor nurses were glaring at her like she was a criminal.

She just wanted to leave. She had stepped out and obeyed what she felt God had asked of her; this was starting to get scary. The guard came back with her ID.

"Thank you," Aimee said, turning to leave.

"You're not going anywhere just yet," the smaller guard said. Apparently this was such a huge deal that she had to meet with the chairman of the hospital; maybe she *was* headed for "visiting-hospital-patients jail" after all.

He showed up, white coat and all. "We have people for this, miss," he scolded.

"I understand," Aimee said. She was starting to get emotional.

"You can go now. Show her out," he said to the big guard.

Walking to the elevator like a little girl being accompanied by her teacher to see the principal, Aimee said, "I don't need to be escorted. I'll go."

"It's just policy, ma'am," the big guard said kindly.

Once the elevator doors closed, he touched Aimee's arm. "Hold your head up! You heard that still small voice and you obeyed. That is more than most people are willing to do. Don't let this discourage you. You have no idea the impact your obedience had on this hospital."

When Aimee told me this story, I was struck with how Christlike the big guard was. On the elevator ride down, he continued to encourage her. As he escorted Aimee to her car, he said something that seemed to contradict everything going on. "Aimee, you are welcome anytime." It's a funny thing to say to someone you are escorting off the premises, but he said it. He recognized the truth amidst opposition. God asked Aimee to go; she was there on His authority.

Aimee obeyed the promptings of God. She went even though it was uncomfortable and a little scary. She apparently broke some rules, and while I understand rules have a purpose, this story isn't really about the rules; it's about risking. It's about Aimee's willingness to step out into the discomfort of obedience. It's about doing it for the story.

Break Some Rules

So rise up, oh Bride of God
Be faithful with your trust

At the beginning of this chapter I noted that I come from a family of storytellers. Well, you could also say it this way, I come from a family of rule breakers. You see the best stories are always the ones that break some rules.

My family, we are not much into rules. Especially the religious rules that box us in and conform us to an apathetic, uninspired existence. You know, the stupid rules. The rules that restrain us to living a "safe" expression of Christianity and remove us from the miraculous birthright we are meant to experience. The rules that limit God and therefore make for a boring story.

I remember the uncomfortable Sunday morning when my dad broke some religious rules for a new story. I was there. My dad had been pastoring a church in Mississippi for over a year when I came home from college for Christmas break.

It was 11:05 a.m. Sunday morning when the worship leader played the last chord. It reverberated throughout the room. Thirty seconds passed and the worship leader looked to my dad, I did too. My dad's eyes were closed and nobody went to the pulpit, nobody took the mic. A minute passed. Dad's eyes remained closed. Then two minutes. The worship team started to fidget. Dad opened his eyes but stayed where he was and still another minute passed. The congregation started to get restless. Finally Dad went to the pulpit. It was past time for the message.

I have fond memories of my dad preaching. He has incredible wisdom and hunger. He wants God's heart more than anything else. Plus he tells the best stories and he is so authentic that you can't help but receive from him.

But Dad didn't open his Bible to preach that day; instead he announced something that changed the Clark story forever.

"I don't have a message this morning," he said. "Let's rest in His presence and trust God has placed a message in one of our members."

If you think that's crazy, what he did next will blow your mind. Against every rule, a heinous disrespect of all things religious, he sat down.

Sometimes like my dad, I break the religious rules because the story is worth it.

Sometimes I don't go to church on Sunday morning. Instead, I sleep in and then make a big breakfast with my family. We call it pancake church.

Sometimes I tip more than 15 percent.

Sometimes I see "sinners" the way God sees them—I'm believing for an "always" in this category.

Sometimes I pray after I eat.

Sometimes I keep my eyes open when I pray.

Sometimes I smoke a cigar. I don't really like cigars, but my brother does, and when he comes over . . . well, sometimes.

Sometimes I stop people in stores or on the street and pray for them.

Sometimes I use mild cuss words to tell a story that my editor has to later remove.

Sometimes I'm late on my mortgage, other times I make a lot of money. Either way, I don't feel guilty about it.

Sometimes I slide our tithe under my neighbor's door instead of putting it in the basket that's passed around on Sunday.

The list goes on, but you get it. Some rules are made to be broken, like the socially unaccepted beautiful behavior of my friend Westerfield, or the rule-breaking obedience of my sister Aimee, or the "trusting in the Holy Spirit to guide the Sunday morning service" of my dad. My point is simply that God loves the good story. The one where we seek the experience with Him and with His people—where we are willing to break away from the bureaucracy of religious rules to know the best story.

I want to live the best story. The kind that you find in the Bible. The kind that my kids will want to tell their kids. The kind that inspires.

> It is abnormal for a Christian not to have an appetite for the impossible. It has been written into our spiritual DNA to hunger for the impossibilities around us to bow at the name of Jesus.[2]
>
> —Bill Johnson, *When Heaven Invades Earth*

Have you ever wondered why, when we were kids, the Bible stories read to us were meant to inspire dreams of impossibilities being made possible with God? And yet as adults, the same stories become observations of how it was "once upon a time." Why is it that the radical miracle stories of my youth found in the Bible have become tamed three-point sermons I could intellectually apply to my life now that I am an adult?

When I was a kid, it was possible for boys to kill evil giants and men to walk on water. When I was a kid, it was possible to live inside a whale, a raging fire, and a lions' den. When I was a kid, it was possible to pray for the sick and watch them recover. Shadows could heal, and the dead could be raised. When I was a kid, I believed that with God, all impossibilities were possible.

The best stories are the ones where life's failures, pains, betrayals, disillusionments, deaths— where life's impossibilities—become possibilities. If you are reading this and you no longer believe as a child, but everything in you wants to, try this statement on for size: "God, I want to believe that with You all impossibilities are possible. Show me how."

Now here's the thing, and I should have warned you first. After you pray this, God's gonna start inviting you to step into your own uncomfortable, risky, rule-breaking story. But it will be good. Why? Because all of His stories are full of the wonder of His good, miraculous love.

Sounds a little scary? Sounds a little fun? That's the whole point. Remember, sometimes scary is fun.

Be Strong and Jump

So give me the land of giants, give me the
  other side
For I am Your believer and we won't be denied

OK, here's my sermon. I'm not on a soapbox but down on a kneeler, all right? Humbly bowed before the Author of the story. Here we go.

Be strong and courageous.[3] There is great risk involved in following Jesus, yet the only way to live the promise, to live a life to its fullest, is found in the passionate pursuit of the Author of life itself. It's not safe, rarely easy, and never boring. It's often hard, scary, and death defying. It's a miracle-upon-miracle, life-giving adventure.

The fact is, God *is* safe. But it's a safety found in relationship; a safety that can be experienced in the discomfort of radical obedience, in reckless conformity to the heart of God. My safety, your safety—it's found in a relationship where we say yes. Yes to trusting, yes to obeying, yes to believing and to taking those two steps and jumping.

I believe God is raising up revolutionaries—men and women who will walk surrendered and untamed lives of worship, willing adventurers living wholly for His glory, risking all to walk beside their Savior. God is growing up a generation that will accept nothing less than a real experience with Him. They want to stand before burning bushes, they want to wrestle with angels, they want to run for the Promised Land and expand its borders. The cross is beautiful to them.

We have the phrase "scary is fun" written on our hearts, and we know we didn't put it there . . . because God loves a good story.

I want to fight, I want to weep, I want to give,
I want to reap, I want to live and believe

Giant Killers

Rock Throwing

There's a cry in my spirit
So loud you can hear it
My soul's awakening

"I'm going to kill you!" he yelled.

"God, help me! Save me!" I prayed.

Wait. Let me back up just a little. You need a little context for this drama. I was ten years old, much too young to die. We had clearly underestimated this guy's speed. He was fast, like "run the 40 in 4.5 seconds" fast, and he was mad. I was fast, but not that fast.

My friend Chris had asked if I thought he could actually skip the stone across the water and hit the neighborhood bully on the other side.

"No way! But I'd like to see you try."

"OK," he said with a wicked smile. Then, not being complete idiots, we discussed the situation and worst-case scenario in case Chris pulled off this miracle.

First, the situation. The kid across the water was a bully. We had once witnessed him knee another boy in the face. In terms of neighborhood justice, this kid had it coming, whatever "it" was. Second, if the worst-case scenario occurred, Chris's house wasn't that far away—only about a 100-yard run through the park and then six houses down. The bully was removed from us by a river, and the only bridge in the park was at least 30 yards in the wrong direction. All we'd really have to do is run like mad.

And then it happened. My normal, neighborhood friend Chris crossed over into the legends of rock skippers. In one singular motion, he twisted slightly, stepped back, cocked his arm, snapped his wrist, and released pure vengeance into the air. It was the throw of a lifetime; the trajectory and spin were such that it was obvious—this throw was the will of God. Time slowed, almost to a stop, and we witnessed the rock dance across the river's surface, finally resting squarely in the bully's stomach. I kid you not.

Alright, I'll cut to the chase, so to speak. Our satisfaction was short lived, all of about a nanosecond, as we saw the bully's face go from surprise to rage. Terror gripped us both. "Run!"

As I ran, I remembered the preacher's joke from a few weeks back, about how when you run from a bear, it isn't important that you're fast, but that you're faster than the guy next to you. Chris must have heard the same joke because he kicked it into warp five or something.

There are moments, even when you're ten years old, that you realize, *I'm not going to make it*. I had such a moment. In that realization, I made a decision based purely on survival instinct. Instead of running down the sidewalk, I dove into a hedge and assumed the fetal position. I lay perfectly still, attempting the old Jedi mind trick: "Nothing to see here, be on your way." But I was not yet a Jedi . . .

The bully suddenly jumped through the hedge, carrying the largest rock I'd ever seen. I don't know where or when he found it, but he had it cocked over his head and I knew this was the end.

"I'm going to kill you!" he yelled.

"God, help me! Save me!" I prayed.

And then God answered my prayer in a woman's voice. Really.

Chris had made it safely home, alerting his mom to the crisis, and she was running up the sidewalk, yelling, putting the fear of God in the bully, while cementing the existence of God in me. A terrifyingly beautiful voice. The bully dropped the rock and ran for his life. Signs and wonders, people . . . signs and wonders.

I have several stories like this from my childhood, oddly most of them involving Chris. As with most boy stories, the facts got a little skewed along the way to accentuate our heroic status. Eventually even the bully-in-the-park debacle was transformed into a tale of epic conquest; Chris's mom didn't even make an appearance. But in all fairness, last time I checked, David's mom wasn't there when he killed Goliath.

Why am I telling you this story? Life is full of giants. They are found in business, education, and family. They can look like financial hardship, or an obstacle hampering advancement at a job. Giants are the things in our life that seek to cause fear through intimidation, or worry through uncertainty; they are the seemingly overwhelming circumstances that stand between us and our promise. In order to move forward in life, we have to defeat them. I believe that each giant in life represents a promise; in fact, sometimes the bigger the giant, the bigger the promise. But the moment God gives us the promise is the moment the giant's fate is sealed. "For from Him and through Him and to Him are all things."[1] God holds the beginning and the end, and through Him, the giant doesn't have a chance. In Him, we were born to kill giants.

But instead of letting God choose my giants, I've often picked them myself. I've assumed I knew best how to define my promise. Using my brilliant mind as a compass, making calculations, and basing my decisions on the fact that the giant is indeed bad and appears to be in my way, I would then analyze the risk, throw my rock, and . . . well, you know how that ends. All too many times, after exhaustion and tears, I've found myself huddled in the fetal position, crying out, "God, save me! Help me! I don't want to die." Thankfully God has shown up with His beautifully terrifying voice just in time.

But when God picks the giant, the scenario changes. I'm not just attacking some random giant but the one God gave me. The question changes from *What might happen if I do?* to *What will I miss if I don't?* I'm not throwing a rock and running away, I'm running straight ahead with heart, mind, soul, and strength. There is no longer any question about whether or not this will work; it's more about how much revelation I can own in the fight, about how fully I can embrace my promise. It's more about what kind of believing I can possess and what impact my believing will have on advancing the kingdom.

A Violent Believer

> *No risk without danger. No faith if I'm sure,*
> *I'm not but I'm absolutely positive in the way*
>   *I'll live*
> *Surrendered and untamed, whole and insane*

His name is Harnish . . . Shawn Harnish. He's been a part of my life since the early Fringe days. He does everything and most of it all at once. He could dismantle an atomic bomb while preparing pan-roasted duck breast, steamed root vegetables, and speckled butter beans for a party of ten, while playing Mancala—the 7,000-year-old Arabic board game—with his daughter. I don't believe Shawn has ever done any of these things, but he could if he wanted too.

I used to think hockey was God's favorite sport, but over the course of a few years, Harnish convinced me that God's game is indeed football (NFL). And after taking me to a Buffalo Bills game, he convinced me that they were indeed God's favorite team. He also convinced his boys of that when they were very young. Now they're old enough for Harnish to relive his glory days through them.

Harnish lives in western New York. Our phone conversations are usually long; we talk about God, church, family, but at some point we talk about football. We talked just the other day; his boys had started football season. He'd told them: "Football is a game of wild abandon, and you can't play scared. You'll never be an impact player if you do."

He went on to tell me that his oldest, Tyler, took quite a hit the other day, and for a moment Harnish wondered how he would play on the next possession. Tyler shook the hit off and remembered the other piece of instruction his dad had given him: "It is better to give than to receive." I love the fact that Harnish is teaching his boys the Bible . . . I also love the fact that he just assumes his boys want to be impact players.

I believe God just assumes we want to be impact players too. None of us were called to be benchwarmers; there is no such thing as a mediocre promise in the kingdom of God. But let's not kid ourselves, we are playing a violent game—life is not all daisies and snow cones. There is evil in this world: sickness, hunger, poverty, abuse, hate. If we want to engage our promise and advance the kingdom, we have to be willing to get violent. "The kingdom of heaven suffers violence, and violent men take it by force."[2]

But what exactly does that mean? I believe it's sorta one-part Harnish, one-part *Polar Express*: "You can't play scared . . . just believe." We've got to be violent-believers.

A violent-believer

- is intimate with the heart of God;
- knows surrender in its purest form—in other words, trust;
- has the courage to risk—sees the giant and says, "You're mine";
- then runs at it with a sling.

Embracing our promise will always start with surrender to God. In that surrender we experience and possess the truths we will need to advance and the authority to run at life with wild abandon. Surrender to God is the most violent thing a person can do. And the miraculous always follows. Sorta like this next story.

The McDonald's Miracle

> *I want to see as You see*
> *I want to dream what You dream*
> *To be what You made me*

Years ago my brother Joel was living in South Africa as a youth pastor. He was headed back to his apartment one day after having been up early and serving a mission team late into the night. Exhausted and hungry, he drove past a McDonald's. The idea of a hamburger, fries, and a Coke seemed the perfect way to unwind at the end of this day. As he walked in, a few homeless street kids stood around the entrance. This wasn't unusual, but as he started to order his Biggie-Size Mac Meal, something else was; he heard God whisper: "Buy the boys some hamburgers."

Joel was tired and only had enough rand (South African currency) for his meal. He was slightly annoyed, thinking, "I've worked all day and I don't even have enough money to get myself everything I want, let alone feed the kids outside the door." But because Joel was *learning* how to live violently believing, he ran headlong into what he believed God was asking him to do.

He bought as many burgers as he could afford, five total. But as he walked out of the restaurant, he saw there were seven kids. He didn't have enough, plus the chances of him getting one were slim. But once you start running toward a giant, it's foolish to turn back. So, he began passing out burgers.

Now this really gets good.

As Joel passed out burgers, more kids from across the street saw what he was doing and began to make their way toward him. Still, he just kept obeying. And somewhere between God's whisper and way too many mouths to feed, it dawned on him that he should have run out of burgers long ago. But he didn't.

Suddenly Joel wasn't tired anymore.

Suddenly Joel was having fun.

When he handed the last boy a burger, he looked in the bag. Yeah, you guessed it—one left over, just for Joel.

I Believe, Help My Unbelief

Jesus asked the boy's father, "How long has he been like this?"

"From childhood," he answered. "It has often thrown him into fire or water to kill him. But if you can do anything, take pity on us and help us."

"'If you can'?" said Jesus. "Everything is possible for him who believes."

Immediately the boy's father exclaimed, "I do believe; help me overcome my unbelief!"

Mark 9:21–24

89

Apparently the disciples had tried praying over this boy who was possessed by an evil spirit, but their prayers had no effect. The boy remained tormented. The crowd waited to see how Jesus would handle the situation. Jesus questioned the boy's father about his condition and got a "please, if you can do anything" response. *If* Jesus could do anything?

What amazes me is that even though I serve the God who created the universe, I still find myself saying "if." What's more amazing is, God knows this and so He provides me with opportunities to step out and experience the miraculous even when I'm not feeling it. Case in point is Joel's multiplying hamburger miracle. With his actions, my brother chose to believe, and because he did, the miraculous broke in. This may not appear violent on the surface, but it is; anytime the miraculous takes place, a "giant" dies . . . and anytime a bell rings, an angel gets his wings—sorry.

The violent-take-it-by-force–believing lifestyle isn't about blood and guts, it's about trusting in His love and then obeying regardless of the risk. It's about living in a way where we constantly cry: "I believe, help my unbelief." Regardless of our physical, emotional, or mental state, God is always inviting us to surrender, step out beyond our comfort zone, into physically, emotionally, and intellectually challenging scenarios so that He can uniquely use us to advance His kingdom.

Oh, and by the way, Jesus healed that boy.

Living Later Now

Faith dwells on the edge of presumption.

Graham Cooke, *When Heaven Opens*

When God gives us a promise, the only way to own it is to live like you believe He's good for it. It's called living later now—at least, I think that's a cool way to say it. We need to live actively waiting, prepared for any God moment. I mentioned that my favorite childhood Bible story involved the boy born to be king—David. Think about him. After he heard the promise from the prophet Samuel, David went back to herding sheep; however, something major had shifted in his heart. He began to adjust his thinking from "I am a shepherd" to "I will be a king." This is profound, as it means he began engaging his promise immediately. And because he did this, when Goliath presented himself, David saw it as an attack on "his kingdom" and he acted as a king should. David whirled his sling, released the rock, and killed a giant.

It's about living later now. David heard his promise and then went back up in the hills to herd sheep. But I think he went back up there believing, living the promise even before Goliath presented himself. This kind of believing allowed David to pull who he was going to be—a king—into who he was. And when the opportunity came to act, he was ready. He killed a giant. The same goes for you and me. We may hear our promise and then go back to whatever it is we are currently doing, but if we can begin to believe, by our words and actions, that the promise is true, then we begin to engage our promise.

Our promises are not guaranteed. They are more like a glimpse of what we can become if we believe, surrender, and live with wild abandon. It's when our promise is aligned with God's purpose that we possess the authority to kill giants; and when the opportunity comes knocking, we can answer it bravely.

Wilde with an "E"

There's a violent hunger in my bones
'Cause I've tasted and I've seen
There's a lion roaring in my heart
And I've determined to set Him free

91

My son's middle name is Wilde . . . Ethan Wilde, with an "e." Karen and I had been discussing middle names for months, and one night while lying in bed, she said, "What about Wild?" There was about a thirty-second pause before I said with much sincerity, "I wish my middle name was wild!" So it was decided then and there—"Wild" would be his middle name. We had no idea what kind of reaction this was going to cause in our family, especially among the ladies.

"You don't want to name him that!"

"Really? What if he turns out wild and . . . violent?"

Personally, I thought that was the point, but we did get some strange looks from family and friends alike. What kind of parents would give their child that name? So we added an "e" to the end of *Wild* thinking that might help the grandmothers, plus it's English and sexy. But in no way do we expect the addition of an "e" to civilize or tame the meaning of the word.

I believe my son will be one of the coming revolutionaries in the church. He will be a man to help God's people redefine the word *wild*, to see the absolute essential nature of being wild and violent in advancing God's kingdom. It has nothing to do with being mean, but everything to do with being intent on pleasing the King and the King alone, daring to live each and every day in a posture of worship, owning God's dreams as our own and pursuing them as if our very lives depended on it. Because they do. They really do.

Divine Insanity

> Surrendered and untamed
> Whole and insane

By the way, did you know God is insane? He searches throughout the world for fellow lunatics. He is always recruiting. His one prerequisite is absolute surrender to His uncomfortable, unreasonable, illogical, impossible, and sometimes life-threatening will. . . . He wants violent, believing lunatics. I know it doesn't say that literally in the Bible, but it's there. Trust me.

Look at any hero of the faith and you'll see they all had moments of divine insanity. Noah to Abraham, Gideon to Peter, Martin Luther to Mother Teresa—they each had moments where they believed, stepped into the promises from God, acted like utter fools, stood toe to toe with their giants, and history was never the same.

I've got to tell you there is nothing safe in believing; there are no guarantees that you will come through with all your body parts intact or that a bully won't heft a rock and threaten to kill you or that a deceiver won't promise you the wealth of the world if you'll just bend the knee and worship him. There's also no guarantee you won't literally die trying.

> Well, you may not know this, but there's things that gnaw at a man worse than dying.
>
> —Charley Waite, *Open Range*

There are things worse than dying, like always wondering what might have been if you'd just trusted and acted or spoken or loved. A life filled with regret has nothing to do with the kingdom. You're either running toward or running away. I'm sorry, but there's no third choice.

Surrendering allows me to live as an untamed, violently believing, God-loving lunatic who is pushing further and further into His promises each day. It's the most violent thing I can do. Some days it's big and obvious, like burgers multiplying by the handful. Other days it's gentle and quiet, like a renewed sense of love for my wife, my daughters, and my son and a commitment to keep on running headlong into the plans God has for me.

Whatever it is, it's always miraculous. It really is.

Relevant

A Goodly Sum

> *I believe the stars are falling, every one a seed*
> *   of fire*
> *And I believe a wave is coming to birth a holy*
> *   pure desire*

We were walking the conference halls and I was feeling distracted, slightly annoyed, and I was trying to figure out why. I had a Switchfoot song running through my head—"I don't belong here, feels like I don't belong." Then I realized that Jeremy, one of my closest friends, had introduced me to a pastor, and this nice fella was talking to me. So I focused back in. ". . . We have almost two hundred members now!" he said, and he was looking right at me.

I can swim from one end of the pool to the other in one breath, I thought. But I couldn't say that! "Feels like I don't belong . . ." The song was still running through my head and Rev. Nice was still looking at me. Quickly, searching my mind, I latched onto the last thing he said. "Two hundred members! Really? Wow! That's a goodly sum!"

A goodly sum?

Minutes later we were walking away from yet another conversation with a complete stranger. Once again, knowing nothing more about the guy except where he lives, how big his church is, how many people are at a Wednesday night service, and how big he expects it all to become. I think he was married, but that's only because of my stellar powers of observation and the wedding ring he was wearing.

"What's wrong with me?" I asked Jeremy.

"What do you mean?"

"Well, I think maybe I'm missing it." That was the best response I had in the moment.

"Why?" Jeremy asks again.

"Because my church has only four members. One of them is married to me and the other three are pretty short, and if I tell them there is a lion in the backyard and if we want to see it we have to quietly sneak out the front door and crawl along the side of the house so as not to spook it, they are right behind me. Or if I tell them that we Clarks have a special tiny hole at the tip of our thumbs, too small to see, but if you put the thumb in your mouth just right and blow hard enough, it will make your leg kick out . . . Well, again, they believe me. So, they may not count.

"So, I guess . . . maybe we don't get it, or maybe we don't belong here—either way, we're weird, man." I included Jeremy in the "we," even though he had said nothing about "a goodly sum."

Jeremy responded with "No, it's just that most of these people don't need to be here."

Jeremy is one of the most authentic men I know; by this I mean he is always Jeremy. He is a worshiper in every sense of the word. He only wants God's presence, and this desire influences all he touches. Before I met him, I think he talked less. He was one of those fellas who didn't like to speak unless it was absolutely necessary. Then we became friends. I really enjoy talking. I'm quite fond of my voice. Sometimes if I'm in an echoey bathroom I'll just start singing. It sounds really good . . . Anyway, over time, I wore Jeremy down, and now he often shares his thoughts just so I'll shut up.

"What do you mean?" I ask.

Jeremy says, "These leaders should all go to a three-day worship conference and just . . . well . . . worship. . . . Most of them don't *need* to be here, they really don't need any more practice on how to do church."

"Here" was a leadership conference for "The Church Leaders of Tomorrow"—at least that's what the pamphlet indicated. We were "rubbing elbows" with attendees as we walked the halls, checking out the conference booths that circled the arena. I agreed with Jeremy; it did appear most of these leaders had come to this conference to learn more on *how* to do Sunday morning, as opposed to *why* we do Sunday morning. The primary focus of most of the attendees was about learning how to provide a better Sunday morning experience. I don't think there is anything wrong with learning better method and I have no problem with wanting to grow your attendance numbers, but as Jeremy observed, the process seemed to be the primary focus.

The conference was a baptism in how to do church better—full-on immersion. There were booths on how to streamline Sunday morning with better PowerPoint, how to ensure better sound, even how to get more people to your church through newsprint, internet, television, and radio. And there were lots of how-to books, which are helpful for getting more "seats in the seats" . . . corny? Yeah, I know, there was probably a booth for that too.

None of the services being offered at these booths were wrong or even misplaced—and I love books by the way. I'm writing one. Entrepreneurs ran the booths and they had come to sell us what we want. But it wasn't the supply that rubbed me wrong, it was the demand. It all reminded me of a statistic I had heard, which probably came from a book. Apparently 75 percent of the North American church believe the worship service is for them.[1] That is to say, they think that worship is designed for their encouragement and for their well-being. That is very American. And absolutely false.

I remember this time, after leading worship on a Sunday morning, being approached by one of the church members. He told me he loved it when I would come visit the church and lead worship. He then went on to say that this particular day the worship service hadn't done anything for him. He was unmoved. I smiled and in my kindest voice said, "It wasn't my primary intention to move you."

There is a line in a Matt Redman song that goes like this: "Let the songs of the saints be sweet-smelling incense to Your [God's] heart." I will often start a worship time out with this song because it properly aligns our hearts understanding as to *why* we come and sing. We come to worship God and it's when our worship is for Him that we are blessed and experience life.

Let me throw this out there as well. God hasn't asked us to worship Him because He needs our worship as some form of payment or because He's an egomaniac. He is not withholding life from us until we give Him worship. He simply *is* life. He *is* Love and He *is* Truth. To the depth we interact and experience Him, we live, love, and know freedom.

So until our gaze is on Him, we aren't worshiping; we're just moving our lips, going through the motions. Until this surrender happens, we aren't truly living. We're just existing, sorta.

These people honor me with their lips, but their hearts are
far from me.

Matthew 15:8

Back at the conference, it seems to me that we, the church,
have been tempted to spend our energy and resources on trying to be relevant. But I believe we have it backward. I think
it's our worship that makes us relevant.

It was a conference on *how* we do church. And that is OK.
Yet my heart aches to experience *why* we are the church. OK
is nice, I guess, but my soul longs for more than OK; I want
God encounters, I want to experience miracles. I was born
to know *why*.

So were you.

Hunger

> *Draw me to my knees, Lord*
> *Make me hungry for more*

Years ago during a trip to Africa, I led a song called
"Hungry" at a Christian school. The chorus goes, "We are
hungry for more of You." At first the students whom we
were ministering to thought this an odd expression. But
when I explained that we as believers needed to have an
almost physical type of hunger for God's presence in our
hearts, they responded by singing with a grasp of the word
that astonished and humbled me. They had a greater understanding and respect of the word than I will probably ever
have. And from their experience, they had deeper revelation
of the word *hunger*. Their hunger stirred my hunger that
night, and the presence of God was sweet as we worshiped
for hours.

I believe the key to encountering God is found through our
hunger. Surrender is what ushers us into His presence, but

99

it is our hunger that leads us to surrender in the first place. Hunger is demonstrated in surrender.

God will always respond to sincere hunger. Matthew 5:6 says, "Blessed are those who hunger and thirst for righteousness, for they will be filled." We are blessed if we hunger and thirst, but there is also a promise of being filled as well. There is the promise of a God encounter.

You know the saying, "You are what you eat"? Well, it could be said like this as well: "What we are hungry for determines what we eat." The cool thing, when it comes to Gods presence, is that the more you eat, the greater your hunger. And the greater our hunger the greater our God encounter. It's our hunger that defines us—what we are hungry for will determine our relevance.

I am learning that God loves filling me up while at the same time increasing my capacity for more.

Healing for Idiots

> I'll live fully to the very end
> Without You it's a chasing of the winds

Jesus healed several blind men over the course of His three years of public ministry. He never did it exactly the same way twice. I'm convinced that He healed each of them differently for one main reason: that's how His Father wanted it done. If there was a second reason, it was probably that He didn't want any formulaic books written on how to heal blind people, no bestsellers called *Healing for Idiots*.

I'm telling you, if Jesus had done it the same every time, we wouldn't need Him. We would all have bought the manual or instruction guide complete with diagrams. Plus, don't forget the twenty-four-hour hotline . . . and online support.

"How to Heal a Blind Man" (from *Healing for Idiots*), taken from John 9:1–6 (loosely interpreted from an Erwin McManus sermon I once heard):

- First discuss with those around you whether his sins or those of his parents caused his blindness. (This should be done in a public place loud enough for the blind man to overhear you. You shouldn't have to talk too loud, due to his hearing being enhanced on account of his blindness.)
- Then spit in the dirt. (It must be a good amount of spit. You may also want a cup of water close at hand as this much spitting can cause dryness of mouth.)
- Stir to a paste-like consistency; make sure you have a good amount of mud. (About a palm full or the size of two robin eggs. This amount is loosely interpreted from the Greek interpretation of the Hebrew interpretation and so on.)
- Gently rub the dirt upon the blind man's eyes. (It would be good to let him know what you are doing so as not to spook him. Also remind him to close his eyes, as he obviously can't see what you are doing . . . otherwise it might sting a little.)
- Smooth out the mud and then tell the man to go to the Pool of Siloam. (Don't help him get there and don't give him directions; if he wants to get healed, he'll figure it out.)
- Finally inform him that he must wash in this river. (WARNING! At no point do you tell him that this will result in him getting his sight. But wink at him when no one's looking so he knows that the odds are in his favor.)

Not How, Why

> *I want to live this life in the brilliance of Your song*

I want to worship You with a life fully sung
. . . a beautiful song

I am having a little fun with the whole "healing for idiots" thing, but I do think we have a tendency to seek out formulas. I am guilty of looking for a principle to the exclusion of an encounter with God's presence. I have read in my Bible about God encounters, and instead of seeking my own, I have often considered, deduced, defined principles, and stopped short of the whole point of the story.

Bill Johnson, author, speaker, and one of my heroes in the faith, says it like this: To know God, we must know His presence and not just His principles (paraphrase).

In the beginning of this chapter I mentioned that Jeremy noted the difference between *how* we worship and *why* we worship. I believe this question is one that every believer needs to prioritize in their heart.

Principles are good—*how* is not a bad question to answer. But we will never fully embrace our promise with principles. If we are consumed with *how* we live or even *how* we do church, we will forever be chasing relevant. If we spend our lives focused on *how*, we will never actually engage our promise.

But if we focus on *why*, we are invited to become intimate with God. We are pressed into relationship with our Savior. We are making strides into our promise. We are, in a word, relevant.

Relevance isn't found in a formula or in a format; it's not engaged in a principle. Relevance is found in relationship, in the hearing and speaking and breathing and loving. . . . Relevance is engaged in the fluid, day-to-day relationship with our Savior and friend, Jesus. Our relevance is defined in His presence.

The Mystical

It's your heart I'm after

If I sought to capture
Would my pursuit be that of a fool

I love holding Karen's hand on almost any occasion. I believe it's one of the reasons a person gets married. It's a quiet celebration of love. It's a sincere expression of forever. Like when you're on a long road trip and suddenly you feel this overwhelming love for the girl next to you and you reach over and put your hand on hers and she knows . . . Or when you are at the hospital waiting to hear some potentially scary news and she reaches over and takes your hand and you know . . . Or when we've had a fight and it's over and we go for a walk and hold hands and we both know . . . yeah, sweeter than tupelo honey.

I also love holding my kids' hands. When we walk through the park or cross the street or pray. When we dance or when I tell them they have to hold my hand while we are in the glass store or the pottery store or the knife store. But that's it, that's where my hand-holding enjoyment ends.

I can tolerate old ladies' hands if we are greeting each other and they don't hold mine for too long. However, I dislike holding hands with "other" people, especially strangers. This is a problem when you grow up in the charismatic church. It seems that most pastors don't truly feel like they have successfully conducted a service until you have taken the hand of the person next to you. And inevitably the second I am forced to hold someone else's hand, my hands get sweaty and I suddenly develop muscle spasms. Or my ankle itches. I mean it really itches! So I let go of the person's hand to scratch my ankle, and as soon as I take the person's hand again my nose itches.

Plus, when going in for the grip, should I go underhand or do I go over? It feels girly to grip overhand. What if I'm overhand with a girl? Then we are both uncomfortable. Of course sitting next to a girl is better than some of the other options. I once sat next to this old man who was in the middle of dabbing a perpetually running nose when the hand-holding unity part of the service came. He didn't even put the hand-kerchief back into his pocket. While still holding the kerchief, he reached out and grabbed my hand.

Speaking of hand holding . . .

I just read an interview with a well-known pastor of a large church. He told a story about going out to look at a piece of property with the elders of the church. They believed that this was to be the place where they were to build a new sanctuary. One of the elders said, "Let's hold hands and claim this property." The pastor, who is a practical kind of guy, said in the interview that it hadn't occurred to him to hold hands and pray that way. He probably doesn't like hand-holding either. He went on to say that he's not wired like that, he's not the "mystical type." *Amen, brother,* I thought, *I'm not wired that way either.* But it really wasn't the hand-holding part of the article that got me; it was the comment he made on not being mystical.

The word *mystical* caught my attention, because another pastor friend of mine had used it recently. We had been discussing how God seems to be moving in our country today. I told him a story about a miracle God had recently orchestrated in my life. As soon as the word *miracle* was used, he shut the conversation down. He told me he was not a mystical sort of person. To him, in regard to the church, emotionalism and coincidence were more likely than the mystical. He went on to say he had seen church leaders abuse the idea of the "mystical God" to get what they wanted.

That's fair. I completely understand his position. I too have met my share of fruitcakes who used "thus saith the Lord" to make up for lack of character. I have watched people make life decisions ruled by their emotions instead of obedience. I am a practical and logical person. If a black cat crosses my path, it's just a black cat. If it happens again, it's a coincidence. I'm not superstitious and my personality doesn't tend to put much stock in coincidence.

But the problem is that God *is* mystical.

Mystical means "of or having a spiritual reality or import not apparent to the intelligence, mysterious."[2]

I don't know about you but the God in my life often fits that description. He is not always logical or practical, at least not in the way I understand it. There also appears to be no such thing as coincidence with God. No accidents and no surprises. His love, His mercy, grace, goodness—all beyond comprehension.

Here is the scary but awesome thing. If we fully surrender our lives to this mysterious God, He will invite us to go places with Him that might even offend the mind. But in the end, oh the things we'll see! Oh the life we will live! John 14:12 says we could see and experience "greater things" than even Jesus saw and experienced. Hey, it's in there, you know. You can check it.

In John chapter 6, Jesus displayed the perfect mix between the practical and the mystical:

> When Jesus looked up and saw a great crowd coming toward him, he said to Philip, "Where shall we buy bread for these people to eat?" He asked this only to test him, for he already had in mind what he was going to do.
>
> Philip answered him, "Eight months' wages would not buy enough bread for each one to have a bite!"
>
> Another of his disciples, Andrew, Simon Peter's brother, spoke up, "Here is a boy with five small barley loaves and two small fish, but how far will they go among so many?" (vv. 5–9)

Jesus's assessment of the situation was practical. "The people are hungry and they need to eat. How much food do we have?" However, His approach regarding the solution was absolutely mystical. He supernaturally multiplied five small barley loaves and two small fish. And everyone got to eat.

When looking at this situation outside of God, the practical solution is either to send the people home or get religious and call for a fast. But what's amazing is that when Jesus displayed the kingdom of heaven's expression regarding practical, it looked like the miraculous, like the mystical. The funny thing is that Jesus was in fact the most practical person within 100,000 miles of this situation. Think about it—what's more practical than multiplying the food?

Also, as a side note, I get a kick out of the fact that John as an author felt the need to emphasize that the fish and barley loaves were small. It's as if he is saying "Hey, guys, this miracle was already pretty good but what makes it amazing is the fact that the five loaves and two fish weren't big. On the contrary, they were small!" Like I would have been less impressed if the fish and loaves were bigger . . .

Here is the thing: God loves to move outside of our logic and into the mysterious in order to provide practically for us. We just need to be willing to embrace Him even when we have to do something silly or uncomfortable like hold the hand of the old guy next to us, though I would like to note that there was no mention of hand-holding in the fish/loaves miracle.

I want to be willing to embrace all of God. I'm up for it. And I'm up for it for two reasons—first, I want the experience, the story; and second, I want an expanded understanding regarding God, the revelation.

You see, I spent several miserable years living without allowing God to operate in the mysterious in my life . . . and I'm never going back there. I have decided to fully embrace all of my promise, and that means I must fully embrace all of God. That includes the God who fed thousands of people with five *small* barley loaves and two *small* fish.

I would much rather move forward into the unknown with a good, loving, and powerful God than live in the now with a packaged, distant, and impotent God. I am willing to risk looking foolish, acting stupid, and appearing irrelevant in my pursuit of my miracle-working best friend, Jesus. I am willing to believe.

It's Our Worship That Defines and Reveals Relevant

Looking down I see my feet
Where once I feared to walk

David steps out onto the battlefield to face Goliath, and I can't help but wonder what the Israelite men on the sidelines were thinking. We know that there were some—in particular, David's own brothers—who thought it was none of his business, he did not belong there, should keep his mouth shut, and stay out of the way. Many of the men, I imagine, were angry and probably had thoughts like "Who does this kid think he is?" and maybe even, "Cocky kid. He deserves what's coming."

Yet I have to believe, I must believe, that there were some who knew, the moment they saw it, the rightness of it—the righteousness of it. I have to believe there were some who watched David take the field and wished they had been the one to step out. I have to believe that with some, the heart was whispering *Yes* even when the mind screamed *No.* I believe this because I have been that man. I have watched while others embraced their promise with a revelation of God and a defiance toward logic. I have watched and my spirit has leapt within me and said, "Me too!"

I think that some of the men, at least in their hearts, knew what relevant looked like before it was relevant. However, I would suggest that David's actions appeared absolutely irrelevant regarding the outcome of the battle before Goliath fell and that there was no one more relevant than David after Goliath died. David stepped out onto the field of battle, surrendered his will, his comfort, even his life, to the Promise Giver. His actions spoke volumes: I am partnered with God and He will be exalted above all else. David committed an amazing act of worship, and his worship defined relevant.

This is a man who had encountered *why*, and because of that, he revealed how.

107

I believe that the measure of our relevance is directly related to the measure of our worship. Again, when I refer to worship, I'm not just referring to worship in song, I'm referring to a surrendered and untamed lifestyle. Worship is the response of a heart that knows love—it's birthed from relationship. And the greater our revelation of His love, the more radical our worship, until we find ourselves squaring off against giants.

What's amazing is that when worship is witnessed at such a level, it commands a response. True worshipers will make those around them hungry, nervous, or even angry. True worshipers will force those around them to surrender and join in or get out of the game. A worship lifestyle radically impacts the world we live in.

Everything in the kingdom of God is birthed out of worship. All of our promises are embraced through worship. Our worship is an act of surrender, our will for God's. But our worship doesn't stop at surrender. When we surrender to God, He invites us into the mystical that is the "untamed." This is a place where we can demonstrate our worship. Show and tell. And as David demonstrated, when surrender proceeds untamed, our promise is engaged and the kingdom is always advanced—victory is always the result. And when everyone gets to partake of your personal victory, I would say that's pretty relevant.

When a person enters into this kind of radical worship, giants die. In this case, David's worship not only brought him personal victory, it brought a victory everyone partook of. It brought strength to a nation. Because of David's radical act of worship, the Israelites won the day. This kind of worship engages a personal promise and therefore expands the parameters of a kingdom. This kind of worship is what we are called to. Worship that starts with surrender but doesn't end there—the kind of worship that thrusts us wildly into the relevant!

Revelation, Greater Works, and Relevant

Please be all I need, please, my heart begs,
*   please be all I need*
If life were a song, come, Savior, come, sing
*   in me . . . a beautiful song*

I wrote about revelation in chapter 2. I wrote that revelation is about knowing in greater measure the love of God. I would like to suggest that our revelation defines our relevance. We can't experience God's love without changing. The more I understand how God loves me, the more freedom I have to live from His perspective.

If you think about it, revelation is about transformation. When we begin to see ourselves from God's perspective—His love—we are transformed. Embracing our promise is about knowing that we are "in the Father" and "the Father is in us."

Our relevance is determined by our revelation.

When Jesus walked the earth, there was no one more relevant than Him. I don't know what He was wearing or whether it was cool or hip to sleep in a different bed every night before Jesus came on the scene. But all you have to do is look at the lives of the disciples after Jesus ascended to see that the "no place to lay your head" trend took.

I am being a little tongue-in-cheek here, but my point is, relevance isn't defined by anything other than doing the will of our Father who is in heaven. It's about being in the Father and the Father being in us.

When Jesus was confronted by Jews who wanted to stone Him for claiming to be God, He actually said to these skeptics, "Do not believe me unless I do what my Father does. But if I do it, even though you do not believe in me, believe the miracles."[3] Several months later, before Jesus was betrayed, He said to His disciples, "Anyone who has seen me has seen the Father. . . . Believe me when I say that I am in the Father and the Father is in me or at least believe on the

109

evidence of the miracles themselves."[4] That Scripture is very profound to me.

Jesus revealed that while the definition of relevant was being one with the Father, the expression of relevant was miracles. What's more, He said that we didn't have to believe in Him if He didn't do miracles. Wow.

You know what the very next verse says? "I tell you the truth, anyone who has faith in me will do what I have been doing. He will do even greater things than these."[5]

Greater works than He did? That's pretty relevant!

I believe that Jesus' life reveals that when you are one with the Father, you become the expression of His will here on earth and that looks like love, like the miraculous. Here's what I'm trying to say, relevant must always first be defined by our intimacy with God before it can be revealed through the miraculous life. There is no formula for relevant because you can't be relevant in your actions unless you are first relevant in Gods heart.

You and I are meant to be relevant—to know God and, like Jesus, reveal Him to our family, our co-workers, and our neighbors through a "greater works than these" lifestyle. I believe that to truly reveal relevant to the world, we must have our own revelation of God. We must be willing to risk chasing a revolutionary God. We must be crazy enough to obey, willing to fail, and yet still expect to succeed. We need our own God encounters, our own God stories. Oh, by the way, this type of surrendered and untamed living? It looks like the "mystical."

And more often than not, these people look like revolutionaries.

The Jump

The Story, Part 1—The God Encounter

I'm consumed 'neath heaven's crush
You are here and You're glorious

I have had several encounters with God throughout my life. Times where I knew without any doubt that God was in the room. Two weeks after arriving in North Carolina, I had one of these. I found myself facedown on my living room floor in the presence of God. His power was manifest in the room—that is to say, I couldn't move. I felt His presence physically. I literally could not move. Talk about a mystical moment. I lay on the floor as the glory of His presence filled the room. He was undeniably God. This was a "burning bush" moment in my life.[1]

During this time, God poured out His heart of love for me and restored my soul. And as always in these encounters, He cemented His promise in my heart. All I could do was love Him more. All I could do was worship Him.

After an hour or so, we began to talk like old friends. It was a wonderfully prolonged time where we expressed our love for each other. I know this sounds crazy, but this kind of thing happened in the Bible, right? Consider when Moses met God at the burning bush or when the disciples experienced the Holy Spirit in the Upper Room shortly after Jesus ascended to heaven.

I began to ask questions about what Karen and I would face in the days ahead. We had just moved to a new city to work with a new ministry without any guarantee of a paycheck, so I was particularly interested in how I was to provide for my family. God responded to my questions with one of His own: *Do you trust Me?* I have since learned that this is a question God will ask every believer who desires to live a good God story. This question must be answered time and again as we engage our promise.

I responded the only way a believer can: "Yes, God, I trust You."

I felt God respond to my heart immediately, saying, "Then stay the course and believe." The rest of the night I worshiped God and He felt as close to me as my own skin. Throughout the night I felt God assure me that He was good and that His provision would neither be a day early or a day late.

The next morning I shared all that had happened with Karen. We had moved to North Carolina out of obedience, and so with the word from God we decided together that regardless of our circumstances we would stay the course and believe.

There is a saying that goes like this—"God is rarely early, but He is never late." I have a friend who says the quote really should be "God is rarely early and . . . well, He is rarely early."

The Jump

I was born to bring You glory, I was born to
  sing Your fame
From my hilltop to my valley I'm surrendered
  and untamed

I have a friend named Joel Carver. I just call him Carver. I think Carver is a pretty cool name, but that's beside the point. Carver is the kind of guy who just knows how to have fun, and he's not scared. I know this because every time we talk about doing something fun, he always says, "I'm not scared."

I had gone to Seattle to surprise my friend Carver for his birthday. His wife Tennille, Karen, and I had been planning the surprise for months. So when I showed up out of the blue, it didn't take long for both of us to decide we needed to do something amazing to mark this special occasion. Well, after a brief discussion, that "something" was obvious—tandem skydiving.

The day before we jumped, I was a nervous wreck. Any time I thought about it, I got queasy. Carver and I began to relate stories we had heard of other jumpers, and of course, eventually the talk turned to the horror stories until one of us would laugh nervously. Then Carver would give his famous phrase, "I'm not scared." Then we'd change the subject.

But once we arrived at the little shack out in the beautiful Northwest countryside, my feelings turned from nervous to excited.

So, as I signed the forms that essentially said, "If you die, or are terribly injured, we are sorry but you can't blame us because you're the idiot that wanted to jump out of an airplane in the first place," I wasn't nervous. As I put on the orange prisonlike jumpsuit, and my instructor strapped on my harness, I wasn't scared. In fact, I was giddy, joking and tee-hee-ing with Carver like an adolescent schoolgirl.

On the van ride over to the plane, I was practically humming with anticipation. And as I stood on the tarmac, I

113

listened with a sense of exhilaration as my instructor ran through the last-minute details. When he mentioned the importance of keeping our arms and legs close to our body so that they wouldn't act as a windmill causing us to spin out of control, I fearlessly joked that we had nicknamed that phenomenon "the death spin."

For those who do not know, there have been times when a jumper begins to spin so violently that they lose control of their senses. They can begin to experience euphoria to such an extent that they actually lose track of time—when jumping out of an airplane, losing track of time is always a bad idea. They have actually found jumpers (landers?) with un-pulled parachutes, which is probably where that joke came from— "Parachute for sale, never been opened, small bloodstain."

When the eight of us climbed into the Volkswagen bug with wings, I was grinning from ear to ear. As we neared the end of the runway, I thought, "Here we go!"

The second we left earth, however, I experienced a terror beyond words. Honestly, if there had not been a girl on the plane, I would have peed myself. I'm not saying I did pee myself, I'm saying I would have if not for that girl . . .

It was a windy day and the takeoff was turbulent, to say the least. The earth disappeared beneath us at an alarming rate. I remember being consumed with two thoughts—first, "Is there any way I can get out of this?" and then, "Oh crap, the death spin." Still, I'm proud to say that I manned up and you couldn't see the terror on my face or hear it in my voice.

If the takeoff was traumatic, when the instructor told Carver and me to roll up the flimsy canvas flap that separated us from 11,000 feet of sky, I nearly had a seizure. At this point I vaguely remember my instructor pointing out the beautiful landscape below us.

"Look at the mountains! Aren't they beautiful?"

To which I responded, "Yeah, they are gorgeous!" But I couldn't see a thing.

My instructor kept yapping. "Look at the Seattle skyline, and the ocean, isn't it all amazing?"

"Shut up, just shut your stupid mouth!" I wanted to scream. But instead I graciously said, "Yeah, it's all amazing!" Still, I couldn't see squat.

Then the plane slowed down and my instructor told me to swing my feet out over the nothingness. *That's the stupidest idea I've ever heard! You are an idiot!* I thought to myself. But I robotically obeyed and whiteknuckled a bar on the inside of the plane. I remember hysterically grasping the irony of holding this bar to keep me from falling out when at any moment we were going to jump. Irony is always so ironic.

At this point my mind had exhausted every scenario in which I could get out of jumping and still retain my dignity. *What if the plane were to run out of gas?* I thought. *No, wait, that's not a good idea. What if I began to have a fake seizure . . . that's it! Great idea, Jason . . . no, wait . . . the fastest way to a hospital is what I'm trying to avoid. What if . . .* But no matter how hard I tried, I couldn't find a plausible way out of jumping. It was gonna happen!

Then the pilot shouted, "We missed the drop. I'm gonna take us around again!" The plane tilted, and for about five minutes I had to sit at the edge looking down at my toes, which at this point hung 11,000 feet over earth.

For the first minute I was in full panic. I started to wonder about my tandem instructor. I realized that I didn't know anything about him. I should have asked him some personal questions, like "How is your home life?" or "Have you been feeling depressed lately?" I was pretty sure it wasn't my time to check out, but I had no idea about my tandem instructor. I pictured myself in heaven, and Jesus asking, "What are you doing here?" "I'm with him," I would say, as I pointed at my instructor.

Plus, were we really strapped together? I mean, I think I felt it. I was 99 percent sure. No wait, 97 percent sure . . . 92

percent sure? . . . Well, you get the picture. I kept looking inside the plane at Carver and subtly pointing to my straps. But he didn't understand and I didn't want to yell, as I thought now was not the best time to upset my tandem instructor by questioning his competence.

Clearly I was about to lose it. Then Carver yelled, "Surrendered and untamed, baby!" And something happened—sorta like scales fell from my eyes. I took a deep breath and began to praise God. At that moment I experienced a peace that was absolutely at odds with my circumstance. Maybe even a peace that surpasses understanding. There on the edge of my demise, I worshiped. I realized this was something I had dreamed of doing my entire life. Here I was, 11,000 feet above earth, and even though I was terrified, there was peace. And it was then I saw the beautiful mountains, the ocean, the skyline.

My tandem instructor tapped my shoulder and we rocked back and forth once, twice—and suddenly I was skydiving.

Surrendered and untamed, baby!

The Story, Part 2—Do Not Strike the Rock

> *I climbed the mountain and got on my knees*
> *Until revival made a home inside of me*

You remember the God encounter I talked about earlier, right? Well, after that, Karen and I began to live financially by faith. Most of my time was spent helping grow the ministry God had called us to, a young ministry unable to provide for us financially. But God had already made it clear that I was to believe and stay the course and He would provide.

Not that I wasn't taking odd jobs, but as strange as this may sound, I wasn't pursuing work during this season. In fact, this was probably the hardest battle I faced as day in and day out I watched our money disappear and yet I felt no release from God to fix it. This opposed all I understood.

116

Before this season, if someone had told me they were broke but they didn't have a paying job and were not even looking for one, I would have kindly told them to get off their butt and go find one. So, as you can imagine, I was in agony.

One day while driving by a Home Depot and crying out to God for provision, I said, "That's it, God, I'm going in there and I'm getting a job." Immediately God spoke to my heart saying, "Do not strike the rock." It was a reference to Moses, who out of frustration acted without the word from God and it cost him the Promised Land. "Then how do I pay my mortgage?" I asked as I began to weep in frustration.

I felt what God was asking of me was absolutely insane and irresponsible. I was constantly fighting deep insecurities around others, particularly church leaders and family as they all knew my financial situation and that I wasn't actively seeking a paying gig. I felt like an absolute lazy loser. I remember sitting with a pastor as he implored me to go get a job. "Aren't you doing anything?" he asked. Another pastor whom I highly respect gave me this Scripture: "A man who can't provide for his family is worse than an infidel."[2] Ah, pastoral care.

But at the same time I was experiencing all these insecurities, I was also experiencing God's presence in a day-by-day, hour-by-hour way.

The sheer agony for me during this season came from the fact that I agreed with these pastors and with those Scriptures. Yet I had heard God speak to my heart—"stay the course and believe"—and this just didn't allow for me to step away from what we had come to North Carolina to do.

I guess what I'm trying to say is, while I was chasing obedience, my experience of God was conflicting with my understanding of Him.

This passage below, taken from my journal, was written during that season and sums up my state of mind well.

I'm desperate, Lord, for you to move on my behalf. I'm guilty and sick, my prayers an old story told too many times. I'm humbled by my need. Those around me think I'm a lazy fool and that you never talk to me. I must see you move or I will die. I'm desperate but still I will endeavor not to be discouraged. I'm hoping and believing *"because your love is Meteoric, your loyalty astronomic"* (Ps. 36:5, 6 Message).

But I've gotta tell you, looking back, this season holds some of Jason and Karen Clark's sweetest memories. There was an amazing peace in our house. I remember at night I would walk through the house and look in on my sleeping kids and the fear of not knowing where they would sleep if we lost the house would begin to assault me. Then just as quick I would give it back to God—"These are Your kids too."

I would then go downstairs and make myself some coffee and I would pour a mug for Jesus as well. Then I would go into my living room and sit down in my favorite chair. I would put Jesus's mug out on the coffee table and then I would put mine down.

You may think I'm a little odd—I probably am—but it's not that I expected Jesus to drink the coffee. That wasn't the point. When you are facing seemingly insurmountable obstacles because of obedience, you need to know God is there, you need to experience His presence. Pouring Him a mug of coffee was simply my way of letting God know I was after an intimate relationship with Him.

Once I was settled, I would close my eyes and begin to thank Him. His presence in the form of peace would come, and it was so sweet. I know you are wondering . . . He never drank the coffee . . .

It's amazing. If you are in the center of God's will, even though a season may be difficult, the peace of God that "passes all understanding" can still reign in you. In fact, you could say that to have access to this kind of peace, you have to be in a situation beyond your ability to understand.

There is a peace that comes with trusting and obeying—a supernatural ability to rest when encountering the overwhelming. Karen and I felt as though we were in the eye of the perfect storm. But as long as our focus remained on Jesus, even though the chaos surrounded us, it never touched us, at least not in our hearts. That place was reserved for Jesus. It was as if we experienced what Jesus experienced when He slept in the boat through the storm. Shaken but not stirred.

For Karen and me, this was a season of the absolute unknown, but it was also incredibly fulfilling, as the revelation of God's love was never more profound, as His presence was never so close. For us, this was a journey of obedience in the face of insanity, and we chose to believe, we chose to obey. The funny thing is, once you get to a certain point in your obedience, choice is almost irrelevant. There is a point of no return.

It's like this. Once you jump out of an airplane, faith in a parachute is irrelevant. It will work or it won't. Your faith no longer has any practical bearing on that outcome. You have gone past the point of return.

And yet, having said that, it was faith in a parachute that got you there. So regardless of what you are feeling, the reality is, while hurtling toward earth, your faith in a parachute is the only thing that matters.

The Story, Part 3—Gratefulness

> *You've captured my heart, now I'm forever*
> *Yours*
> *I give You all, all I am, Lord*

When the propane ran out for the grill, we stopped grilling. I personally learned how to stitch but was still down to one pair of jeans. We had eBayed everything that wasn't nailed down, including all my recording gear. Our fridge was empty and we like food. When the vacuum broke, I vacuumed the

119

house on my hands and knees with a tiny Shop-Vac. "God, do You see this?" I would say.

However, throughout this season we knew we were blessed. You don't have to go very far in this world to know there is always someone else who has greater need than you. So even though we were overwhelmed, we didn't allow ourselves to engage in self-pity. Self-pity is evil. It will shred a believing heart in moments.

God's grace is free—it cannot be earned and we certainly don't deserve it. Self-pity, however, insinuates that we are deserving of something. Whenever Karen and I began to realize that we were experiencing self-pity, we would decide to give thanks to God for all of His goodness, often even making a list of all that He had done for us.

Gratefulness is the key to victory in the battle against self-pity. God is always good, so when we focus on His goodness, it is impossible not to believe. Looking for evidences of His goodness in our lives and then giving thanks always increases faith.

Self-pity cannot exist in the presence of gratefulness. I have seen this firsthand with my kids. We will be driving down the road after having gone out for pizza, after having gone to the swimming pool, after having gone to the theatre, after having gone to the amusement park, after having gone jet skiing, after having flown on a space odyssey through the Dagobah system . . . when suddenly one of them will remember something we didn't get to do that day. Then they will begin to complain. It starts out with a statement something like this: "We never have any fun," followed by a list of things they never get to do. The words "never" and "always" are used freely as one complaint after another is piled on until the minivan (I'm that cool) is filled with a cloud of self-pity.

That's when I bark, "Quiet!" Then, "I want five things from each of you right now that you are grateful for. Quick!" It starts out very slowly as they can't seem to think of anything, so I remind them somewhat sarcastically, "Ahhh, the Dagobah system?"

Finally Maddy remembers something, then Ethan. A little more time and Maddy has something else. A little more time and Ethan has found one more thing. At first they are paying very close attention to how many things they have been grateful for, but by the time we get to number four, the atmosphere in the minivan has changed. And by the time we get to five, we just keep going until eventually all we see is the goodness of God. There is no end of things we can be grateful for.

I told my kids the other day that joy is found in gratefulness, that fulfillment is found in thankfulness. Karen and I are learning to practice gratefulness, even when we're in a wilderness/hard season—especially when we're in the wilderness/hard season. Karen and I are convinced that living thankful not only releases us into joy and peace, but we leave a legacy of full life, health, and peace for our kids.

When we learn gratefulness, we begin to see God as He is. We also begin to see the fullness of what He has given us. In fact, His goodness will become so overwhelming that the desire to give even in the midst of need will overcome us. Therefore a grateful lifestyle will not just impact us but will have eternal significance to those with whom we come in contact. We can only give what we have, and gratefulness increases our awareness of how big God is and, in connection, how rich we truly are.

The Story, Part 4—Ketchup And a Plan

> *I have dreamed and still believe*
> *I have risked and I have lost*
> *But looking down I see my feet*
> *Where once I feared to walk*

"Jesus, please let there be enough money on our credit card to buy this bottle of ketchup," I prayed. I was walking the grocery aisle and I was in deep conversation with God. I repeated the prayer that had become my mantra over the last six months: "God, I just want Your favor. I just want Your presence. It doesn't matter what it looks like. I will do anything, just come and release Your favor on my life."

Suddenly, as I pulled the bottle of ketchup off the shelf, I had a thought. It turned into a plan as I absentmindedly walked the aisle. Six months earlier my dad had invited Jeremy and myself into a new business venture. I had turned him down. For one reason, I was not going to "put my hand to another plow" until I heard from God personally. I was done with good ideas if they were not God ideas. The second reason was that, in my mind, my promise looked nothing like what my dad had proposed.

Walking down that grocery aisle, God gave me two things. First, He gave me a plan of action. Second and more importantly, He gave me a green light. Suddenly I felt an overwhelming excitement to pursue this business. Where six months earlier I would have felt sick at the idea, I was now passionate about it. That night, Karen and I prayed about it and then we decided to step out and start the company.

Only Dead Men Can Go

> *A perfect fear came and claimed my soul*
> *Said this is a place only dead men can go*

Jeremy was precise, his newest victims already forgotten. He was moving forward again yelling instructions. We had the flag in our sights now. I barked at the two kids in front of me as paint whizzed past my head. "Over there, pin them down." I flanked around and delivered the perfect head shot, my last shot. I was out of ammo.

The kid to my left, one of ours, went down. "I'm hit, I'm hit," he screamed. Then to my right, "Hit, I'm out!" It was chaos. With my back against a downed tree, I whisper-yelled over to Jeremy, "I'm out of paint." He nodded. "Me too." He was crouched behind an old tire.

And there it was, our moment of genius. "Shock and Awe"—except it was more like "Bluff and Bluster." We, the only two players left on our team, out of ammo, ran like lunatics straight for the flag, dry firing our weapons all the way. We knew we were "dead men" either way, so we decided to go out on offense. I'm proud to report that we were touched by the paintball gods that day and captured the flag without being shot. We won. This story is one of the greats and will be forever preserved in the annals of paintball history.

In the book *Uprising* by Erwin McManus, he describes a place where only dead men can go. In fact, I wrote a song by the same title. Besides the lyrical poetry, the essence of what he described grabbed me at a deeper gut level. Have you ever read something that just jumped out at you—you knew it was truth but you didn't fully grasp it yet?

The apostle Paul was someone who lived surrendered and untamed for God's glory. Think about the stories that must be buried within this passage about Paul and how God brought him through them all, changing how many lives in the process?

> Five times I received from the Jews the forty lashes minus one. Three times I was beaten with rods, once I was stoned, three times I was shipwrecked, I spent a night and a day in the open sea, I have been constantly on the move. I have been in danger from rivers, in danger from bandits, in danger from my own countrymen, in danger from Gentiles; in danger in the city, in danger in the country, in danger at sea; and in danger from false brothers. I have labored and toiled and have often gone without sleep; I have known hunger and thirst and have often gone without food; I have been cold and naked. (2 Cor. 11:24–27)

God wants to take us to places that will require total surrender. God wants to take us places that will require us to take risks, to look the fool, and to do it with as much believing as we can possess. God wants to take us to a place that requires us to offer up our very lives so we might meet Him there.

I am convinced that it is those who live *surrendered* (dead to themselves) and *untamed* (alive to Christ) who have access to all the promises of God.

The Story, Part 5—Salvation

> *I believe it's begun and is finished, a revolution of the cross*
> *I've awakened to a movement, love my burden, the birthplace of holiness*

It was Friday. On Monday the gas was to be turned off, Wednesday the electric, and Thursday the water. We were not just slightly overdue on these bills—we were months behind. We had turned our bedroom phone ringer off because our morning wakeup call was generally a bill collector. Our credit was maxed and all of our natural resources were used up except one, our SUV, which had been in the paper for two months. Though a year earlier God had promised me that regarding our finances He would provide for us "not a day early or a day late," in all honesty God seemed late. We were afraid. Afraid we'd lose our house. Afraid we had missed it. Afraid we looked like fools.

On Friday I remember telling my dad, "We can now see the whites of the giant's eyes." That was pretty much all we could see. We were at the point of no return. We had committed everything we had and there was no going back. We were "out of the plane." And that's where we found ourselves . . . like David, a mere boy standing on the battlefield, armed only with a strip of leather and a stone, in front of a demon of a man.

When you find yourself in this circumstance and you are there because you chased obedience, there is nothing left for you to do but yell real loud, run at the giant, and sling the stone. For us, in a sense, believing almost seemed irrelevant; there was either going to be a miracle or the giant was going to skewer us. But Karen and I again decided that we would go into the weekend believing.

I received a phone call on Saturday—"Is your Honda still for sale?"

"Yes," I said.

"Great, I'm on my way."

So a guy shows up with cash and buys our SUV. On Monday we paid all of our immediate bills. We even bought a little propane and had a cookout celebration. With the rest of the money, I invested in the business plan God had given Jeremy, my dad, and me. Within a month the business was paying my bills, it doubled the second month, and again the third and fourth month. Within six months it was providing for three families. It was a miracle.

For the Joy Set before *Us*

> *Come let's know our Savior's journey*
> *And find our story in His song*

Just before God released His miracle, I met with one of my closest friends, Shawn Ring, over Chinese. Ring is one of the most successful believers I know, and by this I mean that He is successful at believing. Ring could stand down an army of murderous storm troopers with a toothpick if God asked him to. I've seen him do it! OK, maybe it wasn't a toothpick. I have seen him in some incredibly hard situations and marveled at his faith.

"Well, we are pretty desperate," I told him one day, depressed. "We are pretty close to dead." I went on to tell him the state of things, how we had done everything God had asked us to do, that we were walking in obedience, risking all to follow Him, and yet we were still in bad shape. Or as I put it, "dying." I was feeling a little sorry for myself.

Ring started laughing, his eyes twinkling mischievously. He leaned back in his chair and said, "Well, there's one thing you've excelled at, bro."

"What's that?" I was slightly annoyed.

With a grin he said, "You've been pretty good at dying."

What Ring was saying is that there are two ways to die. You can either die believing or you can die in unbelief. There is a Scripture in Romans that says, "God causes all things to work together for good to those who love God, to those who are called according to His purpose" (8:28 NASB). So, you can either die believing that God is good and that He will work even your death to your good or you can die in disappointment, doubt, and unbelief.

Jesus knew He was to die, to suffer miserably, to be humiliated, and spat upon. Did you know that Jesus also knew that wasn't how his story was going to end? He even told people about it before He died. He knew He would rise from the dead. Jesus knew the only way to salvation was through the cross. The only way to life was through death. And this is what amazes me. Jesus died violently, painfully, quietly, with grace and humility, but most of all Jesus died believing. It was believing that took Him from the Last Supper to the garden, it was believing that took Him from the garden to the cross, believing He would rise three days later, that total salvation would be won for all time for all people. He knew the end of the story. And He died and rose again so we could know ours.

> Let us fix our eyes on Jesus, the author and perfecter of our faith, who for the joy set before him endured the cross, scorning its shame, and sat down at the right hand of the throne of God.
>
> Hebrews 12:2

I want to make this clear. The cross is the foundation upon which our faith is built. Jesus is the cornerstone. But we have to know that it wasn't Jesus's focal point. His focus was on what the cross bought for you and me—the opportunity to know God personally. A relationship with you and me, that was His joy, His focal point. The battle is not the point; the romance is the point. What we must see is that the cross is the doorway to our destiny—it's the threshold to our future, the launching pad to our promise. It's the surrender that thrusts us into the untamed. Our salvation through the cross, although it is the most beautiful of God's miracles, it is not the end of our story; it's where our story gets interesting, because it's the beginning of a surrendered life.

If we embrace our promise, if we live a good story, we will experience cross situations in our lives, but that isn't the end. The end of the story is the joy of greater intimacy with God. It's the surrendered and untamed existence that God has called us all to live. I am learning that during cross seasons in life, if I'm going to "die good," I have to shift my focus from the cross to the joy on the other side. In fact, it's that focus shift that allows me to endure and believe during the cross seasons.

Even at the cross it's about believing. Especially at the cross, it's about believing. First Peter 1:9 says, "Because you kept on believing, you'll get what you're looking forward to: total salvation" (Message). Total salvation is what we are after as believers. It is the fully alive way of life. It's the other side of the cross. It's an understanding that our journey doesn't end at the cross. Our journey, our salvation, is about resurrection.

I love Jesus for the cross. When you find yourself on *your* cross due to obedience, hanging on by a nail, so to speak, you must be doing something right. In the words of a decent song, "Don't stop believing." Really, don't stop.

Only dead men can experience resurrection, baby!

Learning to Dance

The Lawn Mower

I know what you're hiding from
And I know where we're going to

A few years ago I turned thirty and began to have an awful realization. I still fight it, but not with as much blind rage as I used to. My realization was this: I may not be invincible. This thought first entered my consciousness after an incident with the lawn mower.

One hot Mississippi Saturday, I went out to mow the lawn. The lawn mower was giving me fits and I began to pull the cord like I was sixteen . . . and I pulled my arm out of its socket. I fell to the driveway and began rolling around in agony. No matter how I squirmed, I couldn't get my arm to go back in. Grunting and gasping, I could only think of Mel

129

Gibson and the Lethal Weapon movies. In those cinematic classics, Mel Gibson's character was constantly pulling his arm out of its socket, and it was humorous and very entertaining. I remembered that in one of the movies he put his arm back in its socket by slamming his shoulder against a wall.

With that memory as my only reference for solving a dislocated arm, I half crawled, half rolled over to the open garage door. Panting and sweating with the pain, I crawled up the doorframe. Then, in between "God help me" and "s—," I slammed my arm against the doorframe. There was an excruciating pain as my arm popped back into its socket. Then an exhaled string of "Thank you, Lords" as I leaned against the doorframe, thinking this wasn't that humorous or entertaining after all. I was reminded of that Bible verse about "the grass withereth," so I decided mowing is stupid.

As I turned, I saw my neighbor standing in his driveway, looking at me with a mix of sympathy and . . . a smile? I smiled sickly back at him, realizing that it was apparently still humorous and entertaining. Then I waved with my good arm and said, "Hi, Jim," mumbled something about it being a beautiful day, and went inside, thinking, *Is this what happens when you get old?* and grousing at Jim under my breath. "That was *so* not funny!" and "Jim's an idiot."

This was the first day I realized that just maybe, I'm not invincible.

But all of this really only makes sense if I tell you about the triple black.

Triple Black Diamond

For Your glory, it's Your story working in me

About three years earlier my whole family went to Colorado on a three-day family ski trip. The weather was beautiful, with lots of powder and a bright sun. Over the course of three days, I had the opportunity to ski with my sister, Aimee, my brother-in-law, Eric, and even Karen, as Mom watched our kids.

Mostly though, I skied with my brother, Joel. Over those three days, we skied most of the mountain and nearly died a couple of times. At dusk on our last day, we stood at the edge of the triple black diamond. It was our last run of the night, the trip, and the year—so it had to be a good one. If you have never skied a triple black diamond run in Colorado, well, it's almost a religious experience. It's straight down, moguls the size of log cabins, grinning-like-a-fool kinda fun. It's exhilarating.

Joel and I have skied some amazing places, but by no means are we especially good. Yes, we were on the triple black diamond, but that was only because anyone *can* do a triple black diamond. There are no triple black diamond police at the top of the run looking for triple black diamond credentials. And Mom wasn't with us, so we skied it. Why? Because we *can*.

When Joel and I ski, there is no grace or form; there is only survival. It isn't that we don't want to look sexy, it's just that we don't get to ski enough to perfect our form. Honestly, if we could ski better, we'd have to find a bigger mountain, because half the fun is knowing you are in a little over your head. So, Joel and I attacked the moguls, our passion making up for precision. And though we lacked grace, we sure had fun doing it.

As I came to a stop on the edge of a dropoff halfway down the run, my ski popped off. Because the hill was so steep, it continued for a bit before resting at the base of another dropoff. I took my other ski off and climbed down to it just as Joel wiped out above me and lost his skis in the same spot. He climbed down to join me; we were both laughing at this point like little boys who had stolen their uncle's cigarettes. As I reattached my left ski, Joel handed me the other. Both

131

of us were wearing rental skis so they looked identical. The only difference was I'm a size 10½ while Joel is a size 12.

"See ya at the bottom," I said, as I stepped off the drop. I cleared the worst of the moguls and then went into my Olympic form, putting my head down and squatting low. I "let the hill take me." And then, at full speed, my right ski just disappeared. One moment I had two skis and the next I had one less. It just came off. What followed was a wipeout of such violent scope that I think for a moment even God held His breath. Halfway thru the tumble, I felt my arm pull out of its socket . . . a little farther along and it popped back in. Finally I came to a stop.

After a cautious examination of all my body parts to make sure nothing worse had happened, I turned my head to see my brother come to a stop right in front of me. He was laughing! "That was awesome, man!" he said as if I had put on a show. And then, as an afterthought, "Are you all right?"

I lay there while we discussed my injury and the strange circumstance of my ski suddenly coming off. As he helped me up, he said, "It's odd your ski would just fall off, mine is really tight. In fact, I had a hard time getting it on after that last wipeout." I was too hurt to actually kill Joel right then and there, so I just talked about doing it.

Now, years later, my right arm doesn't work as good as my left, and when I try to start a lawn mower, I have to be careful. And maybe I'm not invincible . . . And I have noticed that since the triple black, I ski a little different. If I start to get a little out of control, I experience this odd feeling, I think it's called fear. My mind starts screaming, "Be careful," and though I have heard it before, it's never been so loud or so demanding as these last few years.

When I was a younger man, I prayed some insane, radical prayers. They went something like this: *God! Do what you need to do so You can use me for Your purposes. Purify me! I want Your fire! I want Your truth, Your justice. Make me hungry! Make me thirsty!"* Then with the zeal of youth, I would step off the edge and dive headlong into the future. I would ski with reckless abandon, and sometimes I'd make it without wiping out, but it seems that more times than not, I would experience a wild ride ending in a violent tumble.

It happens. You know, falling down—making a mess of things. Sometimes it happens because someone else messed up. Sometimes it happens because you missed something. And then there are the times it seems to happen for no good reason at all. One moment you're flying high, a shoo-in for the next Winter Games, and the next moment one of your skis will disappear and you find yourself triple-blacked at the bottom of the mountain with lungs full of snow.

I have chased God over so many mountainsides and have experienced more than one crash and burn. I have found myself broken at the bottom of many "mountains." Recently I noticed that my prayers have turned from the radical "Though He slay me I will follow" to the whispered "Lord, I love You, be gentle."

Give a Man a Sword

> *Cover me, care for me, love me*
> *Keep me Yours*

I used to think Peter denied Christ simply out of fear for his own life. But I don't believe that anymore. When Jesus tells Peter that he will deny Him three times, Peter flat-out refuses: "Even if I have to die with You, I will not deny You."[1] When we look at all the Gospels together, we get a good picture of that night in Gethsemane. You know what? Peter told the truth, he did step up. He did step out, even to the point of giving his life. He pulled his sword out and swung it.

Peter didn't intend for his sword to miss. He wasn't just going for an ear, he was literally trying to take someone's

133

head off. I think that swinging the sword was as bold, if not bolder, than when Peter got out of the boat and walked on water. The second he swung the sword, he made a choice to be something other than a fisherman or even a disciple; he chose to be a murderer. He chose to be a criminal for Jesus.

Peter was good on his word to Jesus. "Even if I have to die with You"—that was the decision he made when he swung that sword. We all know Peter didn't understand, but I wonder, was he supposed to? In Luke's Gospel, just before they go to the Garden, Jesus tells the disciples "difficult times" are coming and that they should go and get a sword.[2]

So what else was Peter to do but use the sword he'd been told to get? It's a fairly logical conclusion (if Jesus asked me to get a sword, it would seem pretty obvious that I might be expected to use it), yet when Peter stepped out and used his sword, when he was ready to give his life on behalf of Jesus, he was rebuked. What's more, Jesus heals the guy that Peter de-eared. So Peter, along with all the other disciples, fled. Still, Peter's love for Christ draws him to follow behind, and when confronted with knowing Jesus, he denies Him—three times.

And I wonder, what was left for him to do? When we become disillusioned, the natural response is fear, and I believe Peter was left utterly disillusioned and therefore terrified. I would suggest that it was not fear but disillusionment that first caused Peter to deny Christ. In fact, I would go so far as to say that he had fearlessly defended his Savior, his friend. He had followed wholeheartedly, even bringing and using the sword that Jesus told him he would need.

And he got it completely wrong. He hadn't learned to dance yet.

A Penny in His Pocket

> *Come let's go up to the mountain*
> *Come let's worship beneath the cross*

Come let's know our Savior's journey
And find our story in His song

I was listening to a song recently by Imogen Heap (Frou Frou). The song goes like this: "But then it's your life . . . but you've only got one . . ." I told God once that I would be like a penny in His pocket and that He could spend me any way He wanted to. I've come to the realization that God has many pennies and spends them liberally on whatever pleases His heart. To me, at certain times in my life, He has seemed to be the opposite of frugal, almost casually spending on whims, which makes sense considering He's got plenty of pennies.

The song says "it's your life," but it is not my life, it's His. I gave it to Him years ago and He took me at my word. Ever since, He has been spending me in ways I rarely understand, often causing disillusionment along the way. Just when I think I get it, I experience another failure, one more to add to the pile. I step out bold in my love for Him, and come back reeling from a fist to the jaw. It's like some kind of violent dance.

I have had great ideas in my life, godly noble dreams. Some of them were given to me by my heavenly Father, and for as many dreams as He has placed in my heart, I've had my own to match. I've dragged God along with me on some of these ideas—these dreams that were not completely surrendered. There is nothing more exhausting than trying to fit God into one of your dreams.

I've also followed Him wholeheartedly and watched all my efforts fail. I've gotten ahead of God and I've trailed behind. I've fallen asleep in the garden and I've swung my sword. And I've wept on my face at the only place to fall, a place called the cross.

The pathway God has led me on has at times seemed to me to be counter to His promises. And there have been seasons in my life where the only thing I can say to God is, "I don't understand, this doesn't look good, this doesn't feel good either." What's more, it's almost as if, at these times, God doesn't seem really concerned with me being able to understand.

I believe I will be a part of what God is doing on the earth. It is my destiny. I claim it. It is my promise. I have had the promise since my birth. I've been aware of it for years, and all that time my heavenly Father has been sometimes gently and sometimes violently grooming me. "Whatever it takes," I've said to Him, and I am pretty sure He's taken me seriously.

Oh, remember the lawn mower and the triple black? I still need to tell you about the ledge.

The Ledge

To die with Him it is our journey
To live again and know His love

Mount Finlayson was a favorite climb, close by—it was something we could do in a day. My dad, Joel, and I would start out on the marked trail and in good Clark fashion find an alternate route that was a little more challenging. On this particular day, we were quite a ways up and had climbed our way over to a series of steeply angled rock ledges when I slipped. I was on my back as I slid over the first ledge, about a four-foot drop. I was still a good way from the ultimate cliff edge so I felt that all was under control, but instead of stopping I continued sliding on my back, increasing in speed as I headed for the next dropoff. I scrambled for anything to grab onto but couldn't seem to slow myself down. As I slid over the second ledge, all I could see was sky, and I thought, "This is it," only to fall five feet onto another rock ledge and start sliding again. Once more I fought to stop the slide, but once more I was flung over the edge. (I'm almost finished, alright?) Again I thought I was dead, but there was another ledge. This time I found a crevasse in the rock and was able to finally stop my fall.

I remember lying there on that rock, my breath short, my heart raging. I started checking limbs—nothing was broken, just cuts, bruises, and torn fingernails. On trembling legs I stood and began to climb back to the guys. As I cleared the last ledge and looked up, my dad yelled, "You all right?"

"I think so," I gasped.

There was a short pause, and then he started laughing as his look of terror turned to relief. Then Joel started laughing . . . It took me a moment to join in. By the time I had climbed back up to them, our laughter echoed halfway to heaven.

Looking back, one of the clearest parts of that memory is that, from my falling vantage point, each dropoff was my last one. I died three times that day only to find there was another ledge below to catch me. I tell this story because it has often seemed that my pursuit of God and His promise has been much the same—almost as if God has invited me to know Him through the experience of not just the climb but the helpless falls along the way as well.

I've come to call it the dance of disillusionment.

A Matter of Trust

> God was looking on me battered by the wind
> To see if I would stumble, to see if I would
>   bend . . .

Just before Jesus was betrayed and handed over to the Jewish religious leaders, He said to Peter, "Simon, I've prayed for you in particular that you not give in or give out. When you have come through the time of testing, turn to your companions and give them a fresh start."[3]

Peter gave the typical Peter response: "I will, even if the other disciples don't." Then Jesus, just after telling Peter that he is praying for him to keep faith, says the craziest thing. "Before the rooster crows you will have three times denied that you know me."[4] Essentially, "Hey, Pete, you will deny Me, you will fail Me."

What?! It's hard for me to wrap my head around this. It seems cruel. Why set Peter up to fail? Jesus was already going to the cross. Wasn't it already painful and confusing enough for Peter? Wasn't the test big enough just to be a disciple of Jesus during this time? Why add to the trauma?

In the midst of writing this, with tears in my eyes, I asked God to please show me why this was necessary. And here is what I believe He said to my heart. Jesus wasn't expecting Peter to understand or even "pass" the time of testing. Whether he passed or understood was irrelevant; it was simply that he experience and endure, and learn to dance.

> Never give a man a sword who can't dance.
>
> Celtic proverb

I believe Peter had to have this painful testing experience. It was an absolutely essential part of his story. It was never about his understanding the situation. It could be said Peter failed during his time of testing, but it wasn't about his success, it was about his experience. Jesus already knew Peter would deny Him. Yet the experience was essential to Peter's journey.

After Jesus had risen from the grave and all was said and done, He met with the disciples out on the beach. Jesus and Peter went for a walk, and then Jesus asked Peter the same question three times: "Do you love Me, Peter?"

I think you could also phrase the question this way: "Peter, can I trust you with a sword?"

Peter can only respond, "Yes, Lord. Lord, You know I love You."

Jesus says, "Feed My sheep." With that commission, Peter was released to live his promise fully untamed. And with that commission, Jesus released an anointing on Peter that any believer would envy.

That day on the beach, Peter learned that the sword Jesus had told them about was not an extension of his arm but rather of his heart—that the power of his sword was not found in determination but in surrender. It meant trading fear for God's always good love, trading his self-consciousness for God-consciousness. When you're not self-conscious, you're free to dance, forgive, serve, and love.

God was cultivating a profound revelation of surrender in Peter. You see, the Peter from the Garden couldn't be trusted to live untamed. He couldn't be trusted to swing a sword until he understood brokenness, until he had become intimate with surrender, until he had learned to dance. God was building the foundation of His church upon the truth of surrender that He was birthing in Peter.

Three days earlier, Peter boldly knew he loved Jesus. You couldn't have convinced him otherwise. He was willing to murder for Jesus. A man who doesn't know how to dance is a dangerous man, even if he's a disciple. He might just kill you. However, now on the other side of the disillusionment, Peter not only loved Jesus in brash boldness but in pure brokenness. His ownership of that experience from denial to redemption was what allowed him to be life to his friends.

And that is where our promise lives, within the marriage of surrendered and untamed. Jesus said it is not by might and not by power, but by His Spirit.

Amazingly, because of the cross, because of grace, we can fail Jesus and not be failures. In fact, to think otherwise belittles what He did at Calvary. Outside of His grace we are not capable of loving Jesus. Inside of His grace we are not capable of failing Him. We can get it wrong, but in believing, get it right. We won't always understand the journey, and that's the point. We have to learn the dance steps of disillusionment. God shatters our illusions until our hearts are in full alignment with His. Then it's our joy to run after Jesus, and it's His joy to work it all to His glory.

The wilder we want to be used by God, the more intimate we must be with surrender. And God is faithful in His preparation of us when releasing His power and authority—when giving us a sword. God doesn't think small, and though I will focus on this in the last chapters, I need to make the statement here. *God's plans for us are big.* He has plans so big that to engage them we must step into a greater revelation of who God is. And for that, we'll need a sword. And along the way we have to learn to dance.

So, I've survived the lawn mower and the triple black and the ledge. But I'm still learning about the fire.

The Fire

> *I stood on the edge to see what I could see*
> *Saw Your bride enraptured in the song of Your*
>   *love*
> *In the fires of Your glory*

After a time of worship, Jeremy shared a vision he had. He saw a fire. One man walked up to it, then stepped around it and continued walking. Another walked up to the fire, stepped in, and then quickly jumped out and continued on his way. He said the third man was me, and when I got to the fire, I jumped in and stayed.

I thought about this for a moment . . . I surely was in the fire, and though it seemed I was the idiot in this scenario, I immediately realized that the only reason I was in the fire was because Jesus was in the fire too. And what do you learn to do in the fire? Dance. And why does Jesus want me to learn to dance? He's got a sword for me to wield. It's part of my promise. I believe it's part of yours too.

> Pure gold put in the fire comes out of it proved pure; genuine faith put through this suffering comes out proved genuine. When Jesus wraps this all up, it's your faith, not your gold, that God will have on display as evidence of his victory.[5]

140

Pharmaceuticals

I saw the stars tonight, You were there
I saw them burning bright, You were there

I'm not much of an academic sort. I did go to Bible college and almost graduated too. I still have to write a paper on my senior internship. I wonder if they would accept this book . . .

As a kid I attended our very own "church school," and in third grade I was held back. I found out late in my twenties this was not due to poor grades, as my parents had been told, but to the pastor's desire to see every grade represented evenly. This is understandable. "Symmetry is peace of mind," I always say. There were five third graders moving to fourth and one second grader moving to third, so my best friend Chris and I were held back.

This incident played a role in me not being much of the academic sort. It marked me in a way. It's not that I ever thought I was stupid, but it never occurred to me that I might be a genius. Who knows, if this hadn't happened, maybe I would have come up with an alternate source of energy or something. Maybe. Maybe I would have gone on after Bible college, put some letters behind my name, made millions in pharmaceuticals. But I didn't, and that's why I just had to use spell-check.

So instead of "smarts," I became intrigued by wisdom. These two things are not the same. Though smart can sometimes look like wisdom, they are not remotely similar. In fact, they are often so far apart that if they were in the same room together, there would be a riot, except wisdom would never let that happen 'cause he's too smart.

As a kid I was told that Solomon was the wisest man outside of Jesus to walk the planet. There was one story in which Solomon displayed his wisdom that first offended and then amazed me. I still remember the night my dad read it to us from my very own Bible.

I'm going to paraphrase this story for you.[1] Two mothers were fighting over one baby. They brought the baby to wise Solomon and each said, "The baby is mine." One mother accused the other of accidently suffocating her own child while sleeping. She accused the mother of then trading the dead baby for her live one while she was asleep. After Solomon heard both sides, he simply said, "Give me my sword and the baby. I will cut it right down the middle. Then you can each have half."

I remember thinking at this point in the story that Solomon's solution was incredibly disgusting and terribly wrong. How on earth could "wise" Solomon be that stupid?

One of the mothers cried out, "Please have mercy! Don't kill the baby. You can give him to her." The other mother's response? "Fine, fair is fair, kill the baby." Once Solomon heard both responses, he was able to discern which woman was the real mother. And with that I came into agreement with God's opinion of Solomon: "Wow, that fella was pretty sharp!"

This story had a big impact on my prayer life as a child and through my teens. There were several years where I used to pray for wisdom every day. It was a hunger that I believe God put in my heart, and I'm glad He did.

Get What You Want and Need

Every mystery unveiled
Every secret revealed
You were there

When David dies and Solomon is handed the reins to an established and thriving kingdom, he must have felt an incredible weight of responsibility, and was probably a little overwhelmed. Then God came to him in a dream and said, "Because of your father, I am going to offer you whatever you want—fame, fortunes, just name it and it's yours" (paraphrase).[2]

As a kid I imagined this God encounter was kind of like having a genie offer you one wish, except God is real and I was pretty sure genies weren't. Either way, I knew what I would have said: "I'll have 100 more wishes, please." I remember thinking I was smart for coming up with that, then I remembered being held back and realized I probably just got lucky. I'm not much of an academic—did I mention that?

Solomon says, "I don't want wealth or health or death to my enemies. What I want, what I need is Your presence" (paraphrase). Here is God's response: "Because you asked for this, I will give you all the other things as well." Yeah, very cool.

Somehow, God impressed upon me in my youth that wisdom was actually something you could choose. And I understood that wisdom far exceeded "smart." It was clear that God wasn't impressed by smarts but by a man who was pursuing wisdom. Since then, I've come to an understanding that Wisdom is another name for God. So back to my paraphrase that Solomon asked for "God's presence," aka wisdom.

Solomon surrenders all the other options for God's presence. He meets Wisdom face-to-face and realizes that all his questions and all his needs are answered there. Wisdom is received through a revelation about the nature of God. Wisdom is truth revealed.

Don't miss this, though: what's amazing is that wisdom is always connected to favor. You can't receive wisdom or *truth* without then experiencing favor. Favor always follows wisdom like Christmas follows Christmas Eve or *Rocky XVI* follows *Rocky XV*.

So, what is favor? I'm getting there . . .

"Won't This Be Fun?"

Till Your bride knows Your glory
Till it burns in our soul

First, I have some questions for you about favor. They are a little odd, but stick with me. Here goes. Does a fisherman who doesn't catch fish have favor? Let's go a step further. Is a fisherman who doesn't catch fish even a fisherman? What I really want to know is, what does favor look like to someone who considers himself a fisherman?

I called my dad the other day to tell him about our latest adventure, and we had a good laugh. I had just gotten back from our first overnight family camping trip, which was a new concept for me. It was nothing too wild—a tent, foldout seats, a fire in a pit provided to you by the state park, and restrooms. Having grown up camping in the wild Northwest, I admit I was a bit snooty with Karen about the whole idea.

Before leaving, whenever Karen referenced the weekend as a camping trip, I would correct her. "This is not camping, darlin'," I would say. I like to imagine I sounded a bit like Hannibal from the A-Team. "True camping is a pack, bio-degradable toilet paper, some trail mix, duct tape, and three days from civilization. This, my dear, is essentially sleeping in a backyard tent." I was pretty obnoxious.

But you know what? We had a blast! We slept in a tent. We started a fire and we made S'mores. Plus, Karen, amazing as she is, planned the food, so we ate like royalty. No trail mix—I'm talking steak and chicken for dinner, eggs and bacon for breakfast. Also, we went with good friends and had a wonderful time of fellowship. All in all, family camping is a different but no less enjoyable experience than what I grew up doing.

So I was telling Dad that on our camping trip, I had passed on a sorta-tradition to my kids that my dad had sorta passed on to me: fishing. My dad is not a fisherman. Or maybe he is a fisherman without fish-catching favor. Hmmm. Either way, we have friends and family who love to fish, and therefore every couple of years my dad would get the idea that fishing could be fun. So off we would go with a bucket of worms or whatever bait he had been told the mackerel, trout, or salmon were biting. He would hype us up with phrases like "catching the big one" and "won't this be fun" and then we would spend the better part of a day untangling line with almost always the same results: sunburns and no fish.

As a kid, I hated fishing. I could think of a million better ways to spend a day—Ms. Pac-Man, street hockey, Choose Your Own Adventure, even reruns of *Little House on the Prairie* rated higher. However, as I get older, I too find myself succumbing to the "big one" fishing stories. So, on this camping trip with friends who like to fish, we went fishing.

It was just like I remember it—lots of untangling, sunburns, and no fish. Due to the company, I enjoyed myself, but sadly,

I too have passed on to my kids a strong dislike of fishing. However, something inside tells me that fishing could be fun, possibly even exciting, if we would just catch something.

"[Jesus] called out to them, 'Friends, haven't you any fish?' 'No,' they answered. He said, 'Throw your net on the right side of the boat and you will find some.' When they did, they were unable to haul the net in because of the large number of fish.'"[3] No fish, no fish, and then violà! Lots of fish.

The amazing thing to me is that they appeared to have fished all night and caught nothing, and then with a word from Jesus, using the same nets and the same technique, they cast again, and this time, they catch fish. This time it works.

So what about favor? What's that look like to the fisherman? I believe favor is what happens when God speaks to us. I believe the moment we say yes to God is the moment He releases His promise and with it His favor. Therefore, every promise from God—yours and mine—comes with the favor of God to see it fully engaged. That being said, favor is something we grow in—sometimes for years upon years with little evidence to prove we have it. The Bible tells us that even Jesus grew in wisdom and in favor. Just a thought here: there's pretty much thirty years of Jesus's life—God with us—we know very little about. I would like to suggest that growing in favor often looks like lots of fishing with little to no fish.

It seems at times that I've spent most of my life "fishing" but not much "catching." I have gotten very good at mending and casting nets and sailing. But to be honest, there have been times when, due to the lack of fish, I have questioned whether I was really a fisherman or just a dude with cool gear and a boat.

So the question is, were the disciple's actually fishermen during the long night of no fish catching? I believe the answer is yes; otherwise they wouldn't have been positioned to catch fish on the morning of Jesus's proclamation. And that's huge. In fact, I think that's half of what favor looks like—the fishing without the catching.

I believe that the favor to be a fisherman precedes the favor to catch fish. While both are expressions of favor, there is a growth process. You could say it like this: as you choose wisdom, you grow in wisdom and therefore favor, until suddenly you are a fisherman who catches fish. Catching fish—that's the other half of favor.

So in answer to the question "what does favor look like to a fisherman?" ultimately it looks like catching fish, lots and lots of fish. But before that, it often looks like lots and lots of fishing without the catching.

As I wrote earlier, the promise God gives us is not a guarantee; it's an invitation. To fully embrace it, we must grow in both wisdom and favor until our promise is not just about "a" future it's about "the" present. We are called to live for breakthrough until we are living in breakthrough. We are called to spend hours, days, months, and even years faithfully learning how to fish until one day we catch fish.

Now let's look at it from another angle. We'll get back to the fish later.

Fifteen Years Old, Unmarried, Pregnant = God's Favor

I hope I attain something that sustains
Something beautiful

Sometimes it's easy to confuse the favor of man with the favor of God, almost like two mothers wrestling over the same baby. I'm not as wise as Solomon, but I'm going to try to cut to the truth for you.

I recently heard a teaching by a missionary named Heidi Baker about favor that blew me away. We all know the surface story of Mary and Joseph and the birth of Jesus. But there is so much depth there, especially in light of what God's favor looks like. It is a depth both terrifying and beautiful.

The angel Gabriel comes to Mary in her room and says, "Greetings, favored one! The Lord is with you." And then,

"Do not be afraid, Mary; for you have found favor with God."[4]

Gabriel goes on to tell Mary that she is going to give birth to Jesus. It will be a virgin birth and He will be the Son of God. This section of the story reveals the favor of God in a way that is at odds with how most of us would define it.

Think about this. As soon as the angel leaves, Mary—who is estimated to have been fourteen or fifteen years old—has to go into the next room and explain to her parents what the favor of God looks like. Can you imagine?

"Mom, Dad, I just had an encounter with an angel and he said not to be afraid and that I am favored of God!"

Mom and Dad are smiling ear to ear! Mom, almost giddy, says, "That's wonderful news dear! It so amaz—"

Mary cuts her off. "Mom! There's more!" She takes a shaky breath. "I know I'm young, I know I'm not yet married, but Mom, Dad . . . did I mention that the angel said I am favored? I did? Yeah, well . . . Ha, I'm pregnant!"

What I'm most familiar with has been the "fifteen years old, unmarried, pregnant" kind of favor. It's been the fishing-all-night favor. The moment God reveals His promise to us—the moment we get a glimpse into our future—God releases His favor. And typically that first taste of favor looks and feels a little like Mary's.

Do you realize that the favor of God on this girl forced her to live with the stigma of promiscuity? Mary was given one of the most astounding promises ever. She was honored above every other woman on the face of the planet. She is the earthly mother of the God who created everything. She is the woman who bore love in human form, humankind's redemption in the flesh. And this favor made its entrance, at least to the eyes of man, in the form of shame.

I want to emphasize that God's promise to us always comes with His favor. But that doesn't necessarily mean the favor will be easy to carry, especially in the early days of the promise.

God's favor may look nothing like what we had hoped or longed for. But think about it in terms of Mary. Jesus, the Promised One, was in her womb for nine months before He was born. It took a full nine months of growing and morning sickness and blue jeans that didn't fit anymore—all that pregnancy stuff. Not to mention Mary's bad reputation for being pregnant out of wedlock. In a word—it was hard. But in two words—it was God's favor.

The word is gestation—the process of growing and becoming until it's time for birthing. God's favor? It's about what the Bible refers to as the fullness of time.

I have often said to God, "Lord, I know I have Your favor, but it sure doesn't feel or look like it. What's the deal?" However when I heard this word from Heidi Baker, I realized I have been walking around the last fifteen years or so with the "fifteen years old, unmarried, pregnant favor" of God. I guess some babies take longer to birth than others.

Favor of God, Favor of Man

> Man was made for wonder
> And trust was made by God

> And Jesus grew in wisdom and stature, and in favor with God and men.
>
> Luke 2:52

When God releases his favor on our lives, it may not look or feel like favor right away. I believe the full expression of God's favor includes the favor of man, as the Scripture in Luke 2:52 indicates. As I already touched on, we grow in favor, in our circumstances, our homes and businesses, in every area of our promise. But if we aren't currently experiencing that, it doesn't mean we don't have God's favor; it simply means it hasn't fully matured. I think that when God releases that

149

early favor, He asks us to believe so that He can bring His favor to maturity through our believing.

And so we learn how to believe. We believe even when the doubters say, "You're too young, you need more discipleship" or "You're too old, your time has come and gone." We believe when we are ridiculed for what appears to be failure. We believe while in the wilderness or at the cross, we believe while facing the giants, we believe when those around us have lost heart and turned away. We believe when it's not cool to believe, when it looks irrelevant or foolish or improper or radical or risky. We believe when we feel horrible and our clothes no longer fit and we just can't get comfortable.

Like Mary, we believe and in so doing we learn how to carry our promise to full term even under intense criticism from those around us, including our peers. We learn how to believe in the midst of "fifteen years old, unmarried, pregnant favor." And we do this because we know that the promise is always *yes* and *amen* and sometimes it's also *not yet*.

I am also convinced that when the favor of God comes to maturity, God releases the favor of man. When the favor of man is partnered with the favor of God, His kingdom is exponentially expanded through our promise. In other words, there are fish—lots and lots of fish. Told you I'd get back to the fish.

This is called a legacy, and it's why we are here, it's why we have the promise—to see His kingdom coming on earth as it is in heaven. In the disciples' fishing story, the fish represent blessing and abundance, the fullness of God's favor. Our promise is not only for us, it's for those around us. You can only give what you have—the more fish you have, the more you can give. Our legacy is found in giving from our promise.

There are so many stories in the Bible that reveal this. For instance, Joseph, the eleventh son of Jacob, is given his promise in two dreams. With the promise, God releases His favor and then Joseph experiences the maturing process, gestation—years and years in slavery, serving in obscurity, learning, growing, becoming, staying the course. Joseph continued to believe God, and when the favor of man was released through Pharaoh, Joseph went big-time. He essentially became the leader of an empire.

Then there is David. He is given his promise, and with it the favor of God is released. And his favor? It looked like years of running from a mad king intent on killing him. Eventually God took care of Saul and released the favor of man, and David became king. But not until it was time.

One more thought here. It's important for us to understand that God must be the one to release us into the favor of man. We should not take it for ourselves. Both Joseph and David could have taken the favor of man before God had released it—Joseph when he was tempted by his first master's wife, and David with his opportunities to kill Saul himself. However, both men waited for God. Along the way, we will have invitations to step into the favor of man, but these will be in direct conflict with the designs of God.

However, when the favor of God partners with the God-released favor of man, we get to see a "suddenly" moment. These are holy moments when "suddenly," where we once appeared irrelevant, we are defining relevant. "Suddenly" we are seeing the promise in all its wonderful glory. Suddenly the kingdom is exponentially advanced.

The funny thing is that normally the bigger the "suddenly" moment, the more years of backstory there are. Suddenlys always come on the heels of waiting, of patient, radical believing.

Suddenlys come after we have spent the night fishing and haven't caught a thing. Suddenlys are accompanied by Wisdom's voice calling out across the water, "Throw your net on the other side." And suddenly there are fish.

I want to catch fish. I want all of God's favor. Lately I've begun to live with the sweet anticipation of Jesus walking up on the beach and saying, "Hey, no fish? Throw your nets out on the other side. Now I'm going to fill them up." Now is the time to participate in miracles! Now is the time to engage!

Favor is found when the promise of God is believed and acted on. He speaks, we hear, we obey, and finally there is a "suddenly"—fish, lots of fish.

I Am

No blind eye nor deaf ear
No more wondering if You are here

One of the names of God is "I Am."[5] He is "I Am," which means, He is the God of right now. Yesterday He was God and tomorrow He is God, but I really want to know Him as "I Am"—the God of right now. If I know Him as "I Am" then right now I have access to Wisdom. And I really would like that right now.

Solomon revealed to us that every question humankind is asking is answered in God's presence. I want His presence. I want to dream His dreams. I want my joy found in His presence, my peace found in His will, my freedom found in surrender, my surrender the birthplace of an untamed existence.

I believe that if I know Him as "I Am," I have access to Him in any and every way I need Him—His grace, His love, His glory, His power. These and other revelations are what I must experience in order to keep on believing, especially during those long "fifteen years old, unmarried, pregnant favor" of God seasons. I can trust that when I ask, "Uh, God, are You sure You're still here?" He will respond, "Yes. I Am."

Believing Sows Greater Believing

So sweet to trust in Jesus and take Him at His
word

And rest upon His promise, Oh for grace to
trust Him more

In chapter 8, I told you a story about how God brought my wife and me through a journey in which we experienced financial death. God brought us directly in front of our goliath, and Karen and I both learned how to believe in a new way and obey in that season for our finances. What I find amazing is that our believing was not only important for a victory in our immediate circumstance; it was also sowing victory into our future difficult circumstances as well.

We sowed into our future and into that of our kids and even those around us. Since that breakthrough, we have faced several financial hardships. Our defeat of the first giant didn't mean we wouldn't face others. But our defeat of giant #1 means that when #2 and #3 and #16 show up, we're already walking in a greater wisdom regarding our favor.

What I'm saying is that the believing we do today is the foundation for the believing we will do tomorrow. The faith engaged today makes a greater faith available to us tomorrow.

True Wild Blaze

So we go walking out in this field
To claim our destiny

When Maddy was born, we prayed over her name. We loved Madeleine for a first name, and when Karen suggested "True" for her middle name, we both just knew, it was perfect. She really is True. When Ethan came, we chose Wilde for a middle name. At that point we began to realize that God was choreographing our kids' middle names with what He was working in us. You see, if you live true, you can live wild. If you live surrendered, you can live untamed. But surrendered and untamed weren't really middle name choices. I'm just sayin'.

153

So when Eva, our third child, was on her way, we really felt like God was going to give us another part of the revelation. Just before she was born, God gave Karen the name Blaze and now we have a beautiful little Eva Blaze. What's amazing is when a believer begins to live within the partnership of true and wild, they get to set the world ablaze! When we live surrendered and untamed, we engage our promise. God releases His favor on our lives, and we get to blaze for Him.

This middle name stuff really is cool. It's all tied to conception and gestation and birth and life and favor and promise . . . and God!

I feel I have the smallest grasp of these truths, like a newborn hanging onto the Father's fingers. But I'll tell you this: I'm hanging on for dear life—the dearest life there is, one hidden in the very hand of God. There are stories of men and women throughout history who set the world ablaze with the glory of God. I want my story to be one of those stories. I desire the same for Karen and Maddy True and Ethan Wilde and Eva Blaze. As for me and my house, we want God's favor and wisdom and fish, lots of fish. But not until it's time.

Jason: You're listening, right, God, as I type this?

God: I Am.

11

Calling All Bravehearts

Eggos and Juice Boxes

I turn my face to a blazing sun
Your glory falls, Your Kingdom comes

This may come as a surprise—then again, probably not. I spend much of my time thinking about me. I really don't spend much time thinking about you, unless I'm wondering what you are thinking about me. Of course that would be silly 'cause you're not thinking about me, you're thinking about you. Unless you're also wondering what I'm thinking about you, and if you are, you can stop, 'cause as I just stated, I'm probably still thinking about me.

But when I'm not thinking of me, I do have other thoughts. Deep thoughts such as, can soap really be dirty? Sure the soap's surface can get dirty, but does that mean that the soap is actually dirty? After much consideration and considerable debate, I am of the opinion that soap is inherently clean and therefore it is not possible for it to truly be dirty. Dirt is counter to the very nature of soap.

Also, the word *extraordinary* makes no sense to me, it's a contradiction. Extraordinary suggests that something is amazing. But if something is ordinary, that means it's not amazing, it's just ordinary. So how can something be "extra" ordinary and be amazing. After much consideration and considerable debate, I am of the opinion that the word *extraordinary* should either be discontinued or reassigned for things that are extremely ordinary. For instance, "the surface of that soap is extraordinarily clean."

That being said, one other thing I often think about is, women . . . I generally just think they are amazing. You see, they seem to have a natural inclination to think about others. It's very counter to how I think, and I'm intrigued. For instance, the other day I asked my daughter Madeleine why she loves me—see, I told you that it's usually about me. She had several reasons on the tip of her tongue: "You buy me food, you take me out to the movies, you are nice." Then I asked my son Ethan why he loves me; he paused, scrunched up his face, and said, "'Cause I do."

I totally get Ethan's answer. He is a little man and much like me. It's not that his love for me is any less than Maddy's, but he hasn't recently had a reason to consider why. That's because, like me, he spends much of his time thinking about himself. But we are both learning . . .

Recently, Ethan informed me he didn't want to have kids when he grew up. When I asked him why, he said it was because he didn't want to have to share his Eggos or his juice boxes. "I hear you, man," I said. "Sometimes I have a hard time sharing my juice boxes as well." I can laugh at this, because I know my son and he is a giver. I have watched my kids live generously and they have learned living generously from the same place I have—their bravehearted mother.

156

Karen is the most giving person I know. She truly amazes me on a daily basis. She spends time just thinking about what she can do that will bless the kids, myself, our friends, and even strangers. When she meets people, she starts dreaming up ways to bless them. When I asked her years ago how she knows what everyone wants for their birthdays, she said, "It's easy, babe, I listen when they tell me." I find that to be a truly brilliant statement. She absolutely astounds me!

It's not that they give her a list. What she was saying is, she listens with a giving heart. That means that when people talk, she hears what stirs them, and because she wants to bless them, she is able to discern what would be a great gift.

And her giving goes beyond comfortable; Karen gives courageously. I have witnessed firsthand as she meets someone else's need while having the same need herself. Between the two of us she tends to recognize need first, and because of her we are able to give even when it's a stretch for us. Without Karen I would miss out on some of these opportunities. Karen is courageous. She believes. She is brave. I want to be more like her.

Being bravehearted in our giving is an attribute that God is always developing in His people, both male and female. He teaches us how to see and hear the world around us through His eyes and ears. What's really cool is that as we begin to experience the world this way, we are able to discern the needs and the heart desires of those around us.

Three Stories

> I've been Your echo
> I've been Your shadow
> But my heart is to know You so I can be Your
>   voice

This promise thing is not about self-fulfillment or good self-esteem. Those are all by-products of embracing our promise.

157

The core of our promise is really about God's purposes on this earth. "Thy kingdom come . . . on earth as it is in heaven."[1] That's what Jesus taught us to pray. You know that's the whole point, right? God's plan for earth is to see His kingdom established here, where we live right now. And here's where it gets really cool. He has purposed to use us to establish it. He chooses us! He dreams of a marriage, a friendship, and a partnership with us in order to establish His kingdom of heaven on earth. He desires to work His purpose through our promise, and that revelation makes me smile.

On the next few pages are three stories of God encounters—three different situations where God revealed His heart to me in a profound manner. These three experiences have developed in me the heart of God for the world I live in. From these encounters I've seen that God's purpose is so much bigger than me. Yet He has amazingly given me a promise that coincides with His purpose and wants to partner with me in fulfilling it. These are stories of my heart growing braver.

Story 1: Pandemonium

At the age of eighteen I had one of the coolest jobs ever. I was a roadie for a successful musician. His name was Phil Driscoll. In the world of the trumpet, he is a god—little *g*. He is a trumpet genius! Though I am not a huge fan of the trumpet, I do appreciate talented musicians and also men who know God. Phil is both. I spent six months as a roadie for his ministry, and even though he called me Scott for the first three months, I enjoyed working for him.

I spent most of my days on the road with Dave, Phil's semi-truck driver. Dave was a big man, and when I say big, I mean bodyguard for Hulk Hogan big. He was also covered in tattoos, most of them from before he was saved, so they were a little intimidating. Dave introduced me to truck stops, the trucker code, and steak and eggs for breakfast. (All three of those are wonderfully fascinating and could each be the subject of an entire book.) On this particular day, though, Dave was sleeping in the truck while the crew that had flown in on Phil's airplane and I set up for a rather unique Atlanta gig.

A typical Phil concert was held in a church. The audience would be anywhere from 1,000 to 10,000 depending on the size of the church. There was a simple rig for the light show, a few keyboards, several trumpets, and a mic. The concert would begin with Phil singing to a sound track, his Joe Cocker voice growling out a hymn. Then at just the right moment, he would grab one of the trumpets on stage and begin to play. And when he plays, God smiles.

This venue, however, was a coliseum in the heart of Atlanta. It held maybe 2,500 people. I can't fully remember the context of the event, all I know is that three inner-city schools were crowded into one place to hear the concert. It was very patriotic and had something to do with celebrating freedom and unity.

Did I mention there were three inner-city schools packed into one place? Did I mention we were celebrating unity?

I had traveled most of the night to get there, and my job was to set up and help run the light show. I can't remember who all the speakers were, but I think there was a mayor, a few athletes—one was a gold medalist in the previous Atlanta Olympics—and Phil, who was there to provide the patriotic tunes.

The setup was typical with a stage, small light show (red, white, and blue for this occasion), and mics. The trumpets were put out, the keyboards in place. But when it came to the sound booth located in the middle of the seating area, I noticed that something was different. There was a chain link fence set up around the soundboard with a door and roof and everything. I didn't think much about it. I assumed it was to protect the gear from getting stolen or vandalized.

We finished the setup, and about an hour later the buses began to arrive and in came the students. One school body was seated on the right side of the coliseum, one school body on the left, and one more in the balcony. The show began with red, white, and blue lights flashing and Phil hitting the high notes on his trumpet. Then the gold medalist began to speak, but at this point, I noticed that what was going on in the coliseum around me was louder than what was coming from the stage. The students had stopped listening and started yelling at each other.

Suddenly a fight broke out down front, and I had never seen anything so violent. Immediately a sea of students surged to that spot. I watched a security guard rush over to break it up and he just disappeared in a mass of bodies as they turned on him and began to beat him. I thought someone should help him or at least go wake up Dave the truck driver.

I started out of our fenced little island but was headed off by Robert, Phil's soundman. "There is nothing we can do!" he yelled, and he was right. The first fight was like a match to gasoline; as I looked around, chaos had broken out all over the coliseum. There were fights everywhere. I stood in stunned disbelief as a boy was thrown from the balcony into the sea of people below. People were screaming. *Pandemonium.*

Eventually the police arrived and began to sweep from the stage, pushing the crowd out of the coliseum through the back exits. Once they had passed our little stockade, I opened the door and followed. I remember Robert telling me I should stay with them, but I wanted to see what was going on. As we got close to the doors, we heard gunshots in the lobby. People began screaming and Robert pulled me against the doorframe as a mass of bodies overpowered the police in terror and came stampeding back into the coliseum.

When it was over, I remember walking out into the lobby and seeing kids sitting on the ground or leaning against the walls crying. There was blood on the ground in several places, and I specifically remember one girl vomiting in the corner while she wept hysterically.

Apparently the gunshots were from a policeman's gun. He had been overpowered by the mob and his gun had been forcibly taken from him. In the end, no one was killed, although there were several injuries.

CNN showed up in force with helicopters and vans. They interviewed us. And then it was over. Time to move on. We headed back into the coliseum to tear down the stage just as Dave showed up, rubbing his eyes—"How'd it go?"

Now, I had begun praying at the very beginning of the incident and continued to pray throughout the teardown. In the midst of cranking down the light rack, I felt God's presence on me, then God revealed His heart to me, and what I experienced overwhelmed me. I saw past the violence and excitement of the situation. I believe I saw it as God saw it. And God's heart was broken over the plight of the students. And my heart ached with His and it was impossible not to be moved to tears.

I began to weep. At first I tried to contain myself. I was embarrassed—I thought the guys would think I was crying because I was scared. But I couldn't physically contain the tears, and eventually I openly wept.

Story 2: Lord, Give Me Your Heart

Several years later I was in a prayer meeting. We were crying out for God to reveal His heart to us. During that prayer time, the presence of God fell on me and I couldn't move. His holiness was so thick I could hardly breathe. I began to cry out in hunger for more of His presence. At some point the meeting ended and everyone left except me. I didn't notice anyone was gone. For hours I wrestled in prayer with God. I wanted more of His presence and I wanted to know His heart. My prayer was, "Lord, I will not let You go until You bless me. Give me Your heart."

Suddenly I heard God's voice. His holiness fell, and He said, "If I reveal My heart to you in greater measure, I will hold you to greater accountability regarding what I have revealed. Are you sure you want this?" This question held a profoundly serious tone, and I had a moment of sober consideration. But my heart wanted more and so I said, "Yes, Lord, give me Your heart."

What happened next surprised and shocked me to my core. I don't know what I had expected, but it wasn't this: God opened His heart so that I could know it, and immediately I felt excruciating emotional pain as I began to realize how He agonized with the lost, the sick, and the hurting. I wept the tears of God for the abused and the helpless, for those bound by unbelief. I was overwhelmed with the pain that is daily experienced within our world. And I realized that He felt it all. He carried it all. I also realized that God was only showing me the smallest sliver of His pain, but that small revelation was nearly killing me.

Just when I thought I would die of sadness, God began to minister His love to me. For several weeks after, if I began to think about that moment, I would break down and cry. I would find myself embarrassed by my tears, but I couldn't seem to stem them. The heart of God for His people ravaged me with love.

Story 3: Astrida

We sponsor three kids through the World Vision organization. Karen had a really cool idea of finding three kids who shared the same birth dates as our kids. It was a fun way to make them a part of our lives and include our kids in praying for them and remembering them. Their pictures are on our fridge.

There is Carmalena—she is Maddy's age and is from Guatemala. Grover is Ethan's age and from Bolivia; and Astrida, from Zambia for Eva Blaze. We send a small amount each month to help their families in providing for their kids. We will often pray for them at the supper table or before bedtime.

Though we have never met these kids or their families, we occasionally receive pictures, letters, and information on how they are doing. We received a phone call recently that was terribly sad. Astrida, our youngest, had died.

There was not a clean source for water in her village and so her family had to travel several miles to the next village to get water. Astrida drank some bad water, got sick, and couldn't keep anything down. She died of dehydration—for lack of clean water.

Karen called me to tell me the news. She was obviously emotional. It was hard to believe. There had been no warning, and honestly, we didn't even know that her village didn't have clean water until after Astrida's death.

Several days after hearing the news, I was sitting in a coffee shop writing this book when my dad stopped in. We discussed our business for a while, and then I began to tell him about Astrida. I barely started the story before I was crying. For weeks I couldn't tell the story of Astrida without crying. But I am no longer concerned with the tears because I have come to know that this is a true expression of the heart of God. His heart is broken with the brokenness of this world.

Giving from the Promise

> *Come, oh glory, fill my heart,*
> *Come, oh Brilliance, fill my sight*
> *Every particle of me till I'm a portrait of Your*
>   *grace*

We live in a world that thirsts for the knowledge of God, aches for the presence of true friendship, and longs for the love of a Savior. We live in a world in desperate need physically, spiritually, and emotionally. You don't have to look hard to see it.

Throughout my life, God has revealed His heart of love not only for me but also for the world I live in. As I have embraced my promise, I have realized that to nurture and mature my promise, I must learn to give from it, not to think so much about myself. God has continually invited me to chase Him deeper, and as I have chased after Him, He has begun to grow the desire in me to want what He wants, see what He sees, hear what He hears, and go where He goes. He continues to give me His heart.

God's heart is for the broken, the lost, the oppressed, the sick, the widow, and the orphan. And He desires to have us bring wholeness to the broken, freedom to the oppressed, and healing to the sick. He has called us to father and mother the orphan and bless the widow. The surrendered and untamed lifestyle is learning how to give out of our promise, because our promise isn't just for us; it's for the world around us.

I am learning that when I live surrendered and untamed, God's priorities become my priorities, and when I see a need, I become moved to act. What's amazing is that when I respond to a God-revealed need, I act within the authority of my promise.

I believe that God's favor releases in us the authority to act. That is to say, who we are is now partnered with who God is, in order to meet the need that exists. When that partnership takes place, the impact is not just temporary, it's eternal. It's not just natural, it's supernatural. It's called a legacy.

Often I have responded to need out of sympathy or empathy. And while these can often be good motivations for giving, I am learning that when I act within the wisdom and favor God has released upon me, the impact is not just good, it's miraculously good. The revealed heart of God has an answer to every issue in humanity. I am not an expert; I am fumbling my way along here. But I'm absolutely positive that what the disciples experienced with Jesus is available to us today. Greater works, Jesus said, greater works . . .

As we begin to embrace our promise, we will begin to see with greater revelation the heart of God for the broken world around us. And not only will our eyes become opened, but our hearts will become moved to engage the need and our actions will have the authority of our favor. I believe that this is the kind of living that will change the world.

I had the privilege recently to experience the authority of my favor. While on a run, I came across a girl, probably in her early twenties, who was limping in obvious pain. I stopped to ask if she was OK. She told me how she had fallen and how she thought her toe was broken. She was in town visiting her mother, who was at work and had the only vehicle. She needed to get to a hospital but didn't have transportation.

I could see that the toe was red and swollen. "Can I pray for your toe?" I asked. She seemed a little hesitant but said, "Yes." I prayed, "God, thank You that You love us. I ask for this toe to be made whole right now, in Jesus' name."

I have witnessed others pray for people who have been healed of much crazier things than a broken toe, but as of yet, I haven't seen it happen when I have prayed. That's not a confession of failure, it's a proclamation that I will keep praying until I see healings. And I will, eventually. Why? Because it happened when Jesus prayed, and He said we had access to a "greater works" life. He said all authority on heaven and earth was ours as sons and daughters of God.[2]

In this case, God didn't immediately heal her toe. So without getting discouraged, I told her that I could take her to the emergency room.

I asked her to wait at the coffee shop across the street, and I ran home to get the minivan. While I ran, I prayed that God would heal her toe. While I quickly showered and changed, I again asked God to heal her toe. But before I left the house, I had to make a decision. You see, we only had about two hundred dollars in the bank. That money was meant to last the rest of the month and we were only halfway through. But I had a feeling this girl didn't have any money.

Before I walked out the door, I looked at Karen and said, "Babe, I believe it's in God's heart to heal her toe, but if—" Before I could finish, Karen said, "Yes, we will pay for it." With that question settled in our hearts, I headed to the coffee shop.

When I arrived, the toe still appeared broken. As I helped her into the car, she told me she didn't have insurance and didn't know if Medicaid covered her. I told her not to worry, and off we went to urgent care. As we drove, she asked, "Why are you doing this? You don't even know me." I responded, "Because God loves me, He loves you, and I love you."

When we arrived, she signed in, and she was correct, they didn't have her in the system. I had been standing beside her at the counter, and I stepped in and said, "I've got it." At this point she started crying.

They immediately took her into another room. I waited so I could drive her home. It wasn't long before she came out with her foot in a protective brace.

On the way back to her house she told me her story. It was a rough one. She had been a drug addict; she had been married and then left with her two boys. She had been betrayed and used and unloved. Her life was a mess. Before dropping her off at her house, she again asked, "Why would you do something like this?" I told her the same thing. "Because God loves me, He loves you, and I love you."

She started crying again, and then she asked a beautiful question. "How do you know that God loves you, how do you know He loves me?" That's when I had the incredible honor of introducing her to Love. "God is love, so, to know love, you simply say yes to God." I said. She did. Right there in my minivan. While we prayed, God loved her and she was overwhelmed by His goodness—she experienced God's personal, one-of-a-kind love for her.

I am learning how to love, how to see others and act within the authority of my favor. This girl's life is forever changed. Why? Because you can't encounter love and not change.

I am learning that my favor is engaged when I am willing to risk and trust in order to reveal God's love. Not once did I manipulate her with my actions. She never knew that we used the last of our money for her toe. I chose to simply love her. I was blessed and honored to pray for healing, I was blessed and honored to take her to urgent care, and I would have been blessed and honored even if she didn't ask the question that led to her salvation. My promise is way bigger than getting someone to say a prayer, my promise is about revealing God's love.

It was the revealed love of God that released favor in that moment to share the gospel. My actions had the authority of my favor. And now this girl knows she is loved. And isn't that why we are all here—to know we are loved and then to love in return?

We have been given a promise to establish a legacy of the love of God. This legacy of love is what advances God's heavenly kingdom even long after we have headed home. How awesome is that?

Every Man Dies

> *I pledged my head to a holy love*
> *Put down my paper, picked up my guns*
> *We took the hill, me and the Thunder Sons*
> *We didn't quit till Thy Kingdom Comes*

I love *Braveheart*. I remember the first time I saw the preview at a theatre. I was with Karen at some *other* movie. I actually can't remember the movie we went to see, as it paled in comparison with the *Braveheart* trailer. I kept telling Karen that I wished the movie we were watching was *Braveheart* until she finally asked me nicely to shut up. I saw it eleven times in the theatre. So now you know, as if you didn't by now, I'm a bit odd. That being said, I'm about to go *Braveheart* on you now. Ready?

Malcolm Wallace to his son, William: *Your heart is free. Have the courage to follow it.*

The boy born to be king was furious. David wasn't slightly annoyed, he was mad. "Who is this uncircumcised Philistine that he should defy the armies of the living God?"[3] It is important to know that David didn't just kill Goliath out of a desire for advancement. He didn't just take the giant on out of obedience. Goliath actually offended him. He was disgusted with the very idea of Goliath.

Listen to how he speaks to Goliath when he finally gets out on the field of battle. "This day the LORD will hand you over to me, and I'll strike you down and cut off your head. Today I will give the carcasses of the Philistine army to the birds of the air and the beasts of the earth, and the whole world will know that there is a God in Israel."[4]

David was raging mad. He saw evil/sin embodied and couldn't stomach the idea of it being allowed to continue breathing. He saw injustice in the flesh and determined to destroy it.

William Wallace: *Go back to England and tell them there that Scotland's daughters and sons are yours no more. Tell them Scotland is free.*

Here is the thing. There is available to us a holy anger that will not tolerate injustice. When we see it, we must act!

I believe much of the North American church has gone completely ninny. We provide churches to churchgoers where every corner is rounded and every edge dulled. We have painted Jesus as a longhaired hippie giving us the peace sign, like He is a shy, granola-eating man who sits quietly in the corner, espousing vagaries on love no more profound than an after-school special. A soft man with a title.

William Wallace: *Men don't follow titles, they follow courage.*

168

God *is* love. But God is not ninny-love. That stuff inspires nothing. I know that's not what I signed up for. God's love has the power to answer every question humankind is asking. If we ask for His heart and engage His love, if we truly know Him as love, we will know that He is the most powerful force that's ever existed.

God stands before us and says, *Every man dies, not every man truly loves.* I told you I was going Braveheart on you, didn't I? And yes, I changed that last word. I changed it because I believe to love is to live and anything less is death. Either death now or death later—it really doesn't matter because death is death. But love? Love is life abundant. And free!

I understand there have been abuses where arrogant, power-hungry men have used the word *love* to advance an agenda. They have used the love of God as an idea or concept to herd people like cattle. Both Christians and unbelievers have used the idea of love as a form of legalism and wielded it like a gun. But by now you know I'm not speaking about them. This isn't about the Christian equivalents of Edward "Longshanks" or the talking heads on CNN or Fox. This is about you and me. Men and women who are free.

William Wallace: *Free men you are. What will you do with that freedom?*

Our family, our church, our country, and our world is waiting for believers to act. Not out of some form of legalism but with true revelation from the heart of Love. They are waiting for us to give out of who we are in the authority of our partnership with God. They are waiting for us to get righteously raging mad, maybe even start a fight. They are waiting for us to say to injustice and intolerance and hatefulness and unrighteousness and poverty and disease and abuse and hunger, *Enough is enough! How dare you defy the armies of the living God!*

The welfare of our families, our country, and our world is not in the hands of politicians or even our culture's Chris-

169

tian leaders. It's in the hands of surrendered and untamed believers.

William Wallace/Jason Clark: *Stay a ninny and you'll live . . . at least awhile. And dying in your beds, many years from now, or maybe in your churches months from now, would you be willing to trade all your safety, from this day to that, for one chance, just one chance, to stand and tell the giant that he may take our lives, but he'll never take our LOVE!*

God is awakening us to His love so much so that we not only want to kill the giant, but we know that's what our promise looks like—it's our right, it's our destiny. My prayer is that God would stretch our hearts to give and to quench our righteous anger through radical acts of love, that we would know His presence, and from that relationship live the greater-works life He has promised all of us. The world is waiting for it!

That's what going Braveheart looks like. I hope that put some wind under your kilt.

Bravehearted Giving

> *I put down my paper, picked up my guns*
> *We took the hill, me and the Thunder Sons*

This may come as a surprise to you, but I am learning to think and live beyond me—it's really not about me. I am learning to be more bravehearted—like Karen. I really do want to live generous, both with my time and finances. And I want to leave that legacy to my kids.

Bravehearted giving is how we battle against the evils of this world. Partnering with God and giving from our promise is the most powerful thing we will ever do on this earth. It's time for you and me, the church, to put aside our safe, long-haired-hippie version of Jesus, the one with ninny love, and embrace the man who gave His very life. Giving is what releases freedom. Giving is what saved the world. Jesus has invited us to join Him.

This book is about discovering and engaging the promises of God for our lives. This journey of discovery is about searching out, and seeking the heart of God that we might know in greater measure who we are as His sons and daughters. It's in knowing who we are that we have greater access to our inheritance. Our true identity is only found when we align our heart with God's, and one of the ways we can do this is through giving. Through giving we can partner with God's heart and in so doing further align our affections with His.

I am learning how to live generous through daily and monthly decisions to give. I would encourage you today to find a place to give as well. Giving is your birthright and it's an incredible opportunity to engage your promise.

Karen and I continue to support World Vision with a new addition to our family. Her name is Precious, and like Astrida, she also lives in Zambia. It's the heart of my family to give in the area of clean water, especially in Zambia.

If you would like to partner with my family regarding clean water you can go to World Hope—www.worldhope.org.

Both World Hope and World Vision have wonderful child sponsorship programs. Visit www.worldvision.org.

Find what tugs on your heart and then be intentional about giving there. It's a great place to start.

12

It's Our Birthright

Practiced in His Presence

I turn my face to a blazing sun
Your glory falls, Your Kingdom comes

I was leading worship years ago the day the church had a guest speaker I highly respected.

When I lead worship, most of the time my eyes are closed. So I didn't see the speaker come on the stage and stand next to me. He gently touched my arm. He had a microphone and looked like he wanted to share. I brought the song to a close. At first I thought he would have a word from God for the church, but as he spoke I realized he was talking to me.

"I would like you to take your guitar and step down off the stage," he said kindly. As I did this, he continued. "Now turn your back to the church, face the front." I complied. "Now worship." I looked at him, a little confused. He smiled reassuringly and said, "Pretend we aren't here. Worship the way you do when you are at home by yourself."

I began to play. At first I was a little uncomfortable, I could feel the people looking, waiting. I pressed through. I began to praise God in song while playing a random chord progression. I praised Him for His goodness; I thanked Him for His love and for my wife and my new baby girl. At some point I actually forgot about the two hundred people behind me. Just like when I am alone in my living room, God's presence became real to me. I worshiped this way for about ten minutes. I forgot the people; it was just God and me. I started to sing a song, "I am standing in Your presence on holy ground."

As I began to sing this song, the band, still onstage, joined in. Then the two hundred people behind me joined in. That song led to another and another until we had worshiped forty minutes or so. It was a sweet time, one of my fondest worship memories to date.

When we finally came to a resting spot, the speaker was back onstage. He looked directly at me and said something to this effect: "You can only take people where you have already been. If you go first, you will stir those around you to hunger for a greater revelation of God." A greater love encounter. "You must be practiced in His presence."

Every one of us has a promise that is way bigger than we can imagine. It's a promise that isn't just for us but for the world we live in. This promise isn't found on a stage, it's not about a title; our promise is birthed in the heart of God and is encountered in His presence.

God is looking for men and women who are not worried about being on a stage—those who aren't seeking titles but instead are seeking His presence. We can't take people where we haven't been. We can't give what we don't have.

We must be practiced in His presence. We must know how to worship when no one is looking so we can worship where everyone can see.

David killed the bear and the lion while shepherding in obscurity before he killed the giant in a crowd. David experienced and demonstrated who God was while alone in his "living room" before he ever experienced and demonstrated who God was on a national stage.

For David, it was never about a stage, it was about the presence, and because of that, he was a king long before he wore the crown.

So-and-So *and* So What?

I believe in revolution,
Love's not an institution

A friend of mine was starting a church and asked me to come and lead worship for the group. They were meeting in his home. I arrived early so I could meet the folks who were there, hang out before starting the service, and eat some of the amazing cookies. One of the guys introduced himself to me as a former local pastor.

When it was my turn to introduce myself, I told him I moved a lot as a kid, living in several states and provinces. Often in introductions, when I tell people my history, the next question is, "Was your dad in the armed forces?" When asked this question, I always respond, "Yes. He is a pastor." Sometimes that is enough information, other times I get to explain further.

When I told the local pastor this, his eyes grew big, and with a sense of knowing he asked, "Ah, so is he still pastoring?"

"Yes," I said. "All the time."

"Where is his church?" he asked.

"Mostly throughout the Southeast," I said.

"What's the name of the church?" The confusion on his face was clear.

"Well, one of them is called Clark Hall Doors." I kept talking so he didn't feel awkward. "Yeah, Clark Hall Doors is his company and is one of his many churches." The pastor started smiling—it was a slightly confused smile, but I think he was almost with me. I continued, "Let's see, there's also the Clark Family Church. And then there's the Friends Church, and the Church of the Unbelievers—that's one of his favorites—then he has the Neighbor Church . . . well, you get it."

He got it. I think.

Let's say I'm at a picnic and there's fried chicken and corn on the cob and maybe we have some ranch Doritos. Then someone says, "Jason, let me introduce you to So-and-So" and then So-and-So puts out his hand and says "Hi, I'm *Dr.* So-and-So." I would want to respond with "Hi, I'm Father Jason," or "Hi, I'm worship leader Jason" or "Hi, I'm briefs-over-boxers Jason." Well, you get it, right? I am a lot of things, but none of those things completely define me.

I just want to throw this out there: a title is not for the person who has it; a title is there to serve the person who needs to know it.

Now let's change the scenario. I'm at a hospital and my right arm has fallen off, triple black accident or something. And there's blood and it's pretty grisly. So I'm walking around the hospital with a detached right arm clutched in my left hand when I'm introduced to Hank. My first question for Hank is, "Are you Dr. Hank?" If Hank says, "No, I'm a tailor," then Hank is not the guy I'm looking for. I might need him later, but right now my arm is off and I need *Dr.* So-and-So.

We love titles in our culture. We spend big bucks and years earning them. And in a practical world economy, it's not a bad system, but it's not how God's kingdom works—and His kingdom is coming. Trust me, it's coming. In God's eyes we are defined only by our relationship with Jesus and by His thoughts about who we are.

So when this guy asked if my dad was a pastor, I said yes because my dad can't help being a pastor. That's one of the ways God sees him, so that's part of who he is. The fact is, my dad is pastoral—he always sees Jesus in people and he lays his life down on their behalf so that they would know Jesus more. He is moved to action by others' needs. His flock is spread out across the world and is not confined to the Sunday morning model. It's been years since he had a pulpit, but who needs a pulpit if you've got Jesus? Not my dad.

I'm on a kick for a reason here. This is big.

We don't need a title to see people like Jesus sees them or tell people how Jesus loves them or serve people in Jesus's name. We certainly don't need ordination papers, because God has already ordained us, called us, set us apart. Simply put, we don't need a title to embrace our promise.

In fact, giving people titles that are not true to who they are, not only hurts the body of believers but also the one living under a false title. You can call me *Dr.* So-and So till you're blue in the face. Lead me to a fella who is missing his right arm. Hand me his right arm and the sewing kit. But in the end we would discover to our horror, and possibly his death, that I'm no doctor.

I want to be cautious here because I believe with my whole heart that the calling to be a pastor or teacher as a full-time occupation is wonderful, biblical, and essential.[1] I believe that the community of believers is God's idea, and like all His ideas, it is absolutely stunning. Sunday morning is beautiful, or at least it should be. But hear me, it's not the full expression of Gods kingdom here on earth. And it certainly isn't what most of our promises look like.

Our Promise Is Our Ministry

I had a dream tonight and You were there
A bride in brilliant white and You were there

When I was in China, I met with an amazing believer. He had moved there thirty years earlier with a vision to share the love of Jesus with the Chinese people. Due to the fact that China is a communist country, it was closed off to the gospel and therefore he couldn't live in China as a "mission-ary," nor could he speak too openly about Jesus. So God led him to engage his promise through becoming a businessman.

As we sat and talked one afternoon over eel, chicken heads, and duck feet, among other wonderful exotic entrees that I can only begin to guess at, he gave me a truth from his life experience. He said, "Believers are not saved to advance the church; we are saved to advance God's kingdom. Our promise is to establish His kingdom 'on earth as it is in heaven.'" He then went on to say that there are several ways to see this done.

In the US, the institution of church has traditionally been the vehicle that has advanced God's kingdom. Not so in China. At least for this man, it has been through his busi-ness that he has seen God's kingdom coming. This revelation was more profound due to the fact that he had just taken me on a tour of one of his factories, which was home to 400-plus workers, of which 80 percent were believers. This is an amazing percentage in any country, but in China, it's beyond amazing. It's miraculous.

Then he told me story after story of his employees preach-ing the gospel to their community, of the miracles and heal-ings taking place in the city where his company is located. He told stories of churches being started and strengthened by his believing employees. There were even stories of gov-ernment officials being saved due to the impact his company has had on the city.

Then we saw the awards that had been given to the company. Over the last nine years they had consistently won the award for the best place to work in that city. He told us of a health plan they had put together for the employees, which is something unheard of in China. On top of that, I went to an orphanage, partially funded by the missionary/businessman's company, where I wept joyfully to see special needs children loved.

In China, the government has restricted couples to one child. Therefore if a child is born with medical issues, it is not unusual for them to be abandoned. These children, if they are found and survive, are given to the state and then grow up with little human contact; they live unloved in an institution. I heard horror stories of how they are treated. Stories that would both break your heart and make you furious.

But I witnessed an orphanage where "undercover" believers have been invited to come in and partner with the state. I had the opportunity to see the results: beautiful kids, eyes bright, laughing and learning—one worker per child, another miracle. The workers there were radically in love with God; it was evident in how they loved the children. It was amazing.

Now, get this. Not only is this company profoundly changing their city, the company is also profitable!

It was absolutely amazing! What I saw was the kingdom of God being advanced through a believer's company. It was the church in business the way I've never seen it before, the way I think it was always meant to be.

This truth impacted me greatly because it put words to a frustration that had been growing in me since early adulthood. We live in a country that still believes church is a Sunday morning experience. Even with all the emergent whatever it is, that's still the prevailing view in the good old US of A. But that's not the church. The church is you and me advancing God's kingdom through our promises, both as individuals but also as families and companies.

Our promise doesn't have to fit within the context of Sunday morning to be validated as ministry. Our promise *is* our ministry, and every one of us has one. Hear me, we all have a ministry. Regardless of the title, we are all ministers. Our promises are no less profound or relevant if they land us outside of a full-time position at a church. We came into relationship with God to advance His kingdom through our promise, and so it should look as varied and unique as the

179

hand is to the nose is to the hip is to the eye. We are one body, one church, and no two of us are the same.

Swimming Against the Stream

Let's go find this Kingdom come, well done

When I was five years old, my dad and mom were asked by my kindergarten teacher to come in to discuss my behavior. Now, I can't remember much from kindergarten. There were the monkey-bar fights, where two boys hung from the bars by their hands and tried to wrap their legs around the others torso and yank them off the bars.

I remember "smash-up derby," where all the boys would put their arms down at their sides and then run at each other as fast as we could, trying to knock each other down while making car noises.

I remember hanging from my jeans belt loop off the top of the swing set pretending that I was superman and that I could fly. Eventually the belt loops would tear. The last time I played this game, I wasn't quick enough to grab the bar, and the fall resulted in me getting my wind knocked out.

And I remember my mom wondering aloud why my belt loops kept tearing.

And I remember not having a clue. Stupid jeans.

But apparently along with all my painful landings, I was quite the preacher as well. It seems I didn't like my classmates living in ignorance, and I felt it was important that they knew Jesus was real and Santa Claus wasn't. Yep, I was that kid. And apparently my teacher thought it was the other way around, which is why he called my parents in.

The teacher told my parents that I was "very different" from the other kids in that I spoke about God as if I knew Him. He said that it was causing me not to fit in. The teacher then used an analogy that has stayed with me most of my life. He said I was swimming against the stream. My beautiful father responded, "Yes, that's exactly what he is doing and I pray he never quits."

My dad spoke that over my life when I was just five years old. Looking back, it truly was prophetic, because that has been one of the determining characteristics molding me into who I am today. For most of my adult life, I have found myself swimming not just against a worldly current but also often counter to "religious culture."

What's in a Name?

Love's not an institution

By the time I finished Bible college, I'd had my fill of institution. It wasn't the college, because it's a wonderful school and God led me there. But at the time, I couldn't make the clothes of a pastor or worship leader fit. Does that make sense? It was like David trying to wear Saul's armor. I couldn't even make the title work. And so I continued my five-year-old destiny—swimming against the stream.

With school finished I had begun dreaming of Jesus and rock 'n' roll. Soon I was in a band. I remember the night we named it. My bandmates, our wives, and I sat around the kitchen table, and over empty spaghetti plates, we began discussing possible names for our newly formed group. "Fringe" was one of the first offerings and in the end the name that I thought fit the best. At the time, I truly felt like I was a member of the fringe. Especially in regard to the church.

Our first studio album was called *For the Vagabond Believer*. Looking back, that's what we were—vagabonds, homeless wanderers walking through our small slice of the world, telling the truth to any who would listen. Though it sounds romantic, it's actually quite lonely.

However, in the last five years or so, I have begun to see that my God isn't just a fringe God. He is right at the center

181

of things; in fact, He *is* the center. I have started to realize that my promise isn't about leaving the culture but finding it, creating it, reforming it. That promise isn't unique to me—I believe it is the call of every believer.

I no longer desire to be on the fringe, yet neither will I try to fit a mold. I've come to see there's swimming against the stream just to swim against the stream. And then there's swimming against the stream like the salmon do—to give life so others might live . . . and to get back home. You face predators along the way and the trip is exhausting and you die a thousand deaths, but you do it for the glory and the story.

When this book was picked up, the publisher asked for a subtitle and I chose *A Field Guide for the Vagabond Believer* for two reasons. First, it has a cool ring to it, but second and mostly, I believe that like myself, there are fringe believers throughout the world who have been given huge promises but haven't known how to engage them. We know there is "more" but haven't known how to get there. We have tried to work within the confines of a model of Christianity called Sunday morning and in the end have found ourselves, like vagabonds, wandering the planet in search of a place to give, to grow, and ultimately to know God's love and design for our lives.

But there's more than one way to swim.

The church is meant to release the kingdom of God into the world. You and I are the church. Sunday morning services are only one way to swim. God desires the kingdom to break into education, the arts and entertainment, our government. He wants kingdom-minded businessmen, and so on. A church deep and wide.

> I'm an artist who is a Christian. I'm not a Christian artist.
>
> Johnny Cash

You see, there is no such thing as Christian music; there are only musicians who are Christians. There is no such thing as

Christian books; there are only writers who are Christians. There is no such thing as Christian business; there are only businessmen who are Christians. There is no such thing as Christian education; there are only teachers who are Christians.

It is time for God's church to swim against the stream in all of our promised glory. We were not meant to live on the fringe. We were not meant to run from the culture. We are meant to lead it. We are called to reformation until the glory of God is revealed through His church, His people.

I believe we were never meant to build a subculture but to reform the one we live in. We were never meant to hide out and wait for the King's return. We were born to co-labor with Him and create the world He will return to.

Sure, there are days when that's hard to believe, but we've got to remember—things are not what they seem.

We Are the Giants

> As Your glory cloud descends,
> Hey, friends, it's time that we got going

When David stepped out on the battlefield, the perception everyone else experienced was in fact not reality. To the outsiders, it appeared that David was just a boy, small and weak in comparison to Goliath. But David perceived a greater reality—God's reality. It is a reality that is unseen; it has to be lived by faith. And in God's story, we are the giants. We have already won.

It's time we came to an understanding of a higher reality, a greater truth. Much of the church has been hiding as if we didn't have the King of Kings in our heart. But this world is ours. We are the giants. It may not look like it, it may not feel like it, but it is the truth. Often we have painted ourselves as spiritual dwarfs when God has said we are spiritual giants. The Bible says, "Greater is He that is in me than he that is

183

in the world."[2] There is a way of living that risks it all on the revelation that God has given us the land to take, that darkness always flees when light arrives.

I'm convinced that God is looking for surrendered and untamed believers who know Him, trust Him, obey Him, and then risk everything to bring heaven to earth; those who are practiced in His presence. We can be the worshipers who make breakthrough available for everyone else. David's victory was everyone's victory.

I'm speaking big here because there is no other option. Romans 8:19 says, "Creation waits in eager expectation for the sons of God to be revealed." The sons of God? Yep, you got it—that's us. We are the giants. When we begin to walk in a revelation of the overwhelming love of Christ Jesus, we begin to embrace the authority He died to give us. "If God is for us, who can be against us? He who did not spare his own Son, but gave him up for us all—how will he not also, along with him, graciously give us all things?"[3]

God's love is the most powerful thing in the world, and it's also the most beautiful. Its power is displayed in Jesus's resurrection. Its beauty is revealed in the lives of those who journey with God. We have access to a heavenly truth that we have only begun to understand. We have barely scratched the surface of our glorious promise.

I am absolutely convinced that we have not yet seen in this earth the full wonders of God's love. It's time to live surrendered and untamed. It's time to wake the sleeping giant within. It's time to believe the promise He's given each and every one of us. It's time to stand on the promises and then run headlong into the kingdom that is coming. It is His kingdom, but because of who we are, it is ours as well. It is our birthright.

So won't you join me? Like my brother Joel says, "Do it for the story." And for the glory. The glory of the King.

Surrendered and untamed, baby!

The Beginning . . .

Notes

Foreword

1. John 14:12.
2. Romans 8:31–32.

Chapter 1 The Promise

1. John 14:12.
2. See Hebrews 11:1.

Chapter 2 He Loves Me Best

1. Sam-I-am, in Dr. Seuss, *Green Eggs and Ham* (New York: Random House, 1960), 24 (punctuation altered).
2. See Jeremiah 29:11.
3. See 1 Corinthians 13:4–7.

Chapter 3 Monday Morning

1. 1 Samuel 16:13 Message.
2. Gary Hassig, *CBA Retailers+Resources* magazine.
3. Kristine Brown, Diganote.
4. Mark Fisher, 1340 Mag.
5. Matthew 3:17 NASB.

Chapter 4 The Believe Switch

1. See Romans 12:2.

2. Ibid.
3. See Acts 20:22–23.
4. Acts 21:12–13 Message.
5. Oswald Chambers, "The Eternal God," *My Utmost for His Highest* (Grand Rapids: Zondervan), Nov 17.

Chapter 5 Do It for the Story

1. See 2 Samuel 6:14.
2. Bill Johnson, *When Heaven Invades Earth* (Shippensburg, PA: Destiny Image Publishers, 2005), 5.
3. See Joshua 1:6.

Chapter 6 Giant Killers

1. Romans 11:36 NASB.
2. Matthew 11:12.

Chapter 7 Relevant

1. George Barna, *Revolution* (Carol Stream, IL: Tyndale, 2005), 31–32.
2. *American Heritage Dictionary*, s.v. "mystical."
3. John 10:37–38.
4. John 14:9, 11.
5. John 14:12.

Chapter 8 The Jump

1. Exodus 3.
2. See 1 Timothy 5:8.

Chapter 9 Learning to Dance

1. Matthew 26:35 NASB.
2. Luke 22:7–38.
3. Luke 22:32 Message.
4. Luke 22:34 Message.
5. 1 Peter 1:6–7 Message.

Chapter 10 Favor

1. 1 Kings 3:16–28.
2. 1 Kings 3:1–15.

3. John 21:5–6.
4. Luke 1:28, 30 NASB.
5. Exodus 3:14.

Chapter 11 Calling All Bravehearts

1. Matthew 6:10 KJV.
2. See Matthew 28:18.
3. 1 Samuel 17:26.
4. 1 Samuel 17:46.

Chapter 12 It's Our Birthright

1. Ephesians 4:11–13.
2. See 1 John 4:4.
3. Romans 8:31–32.

Acknowledgments

Thanks to:

God, Your love is so good! That I would know more . . .

Karen, my best friend. Maddy, Ethan, and Eva, you're my favorites! My parents who've always modeled believing, I can't help but love God more because of how you both live—thank you! Aimee and Eric, Joel and Megan, Josiah and Ben. You guys are the best family ever, I love our story! JV, Cindy, Kathleen, Aaron, and Bobby. Thanks for your love!

Joel, for dreaming with me and never doubting. You've *almost* paid me back for all that candy I bought you when we were kids.

Jeremy Cole, the great encourager. Shawn Ring, the great visionary, Joel Carver, the great adventurer. The Rings, Carvers, Coles, Perrys, and Harnishes—men and families with Kingdom influence. All the friends who have been life to my family and me over the years. We love you guys!

Those I would like to hang out with more, Randy Everett, Nicholas Costaras, Alex Harris, and Mark Batterson. Thanks for adding your revelation and helping make Surrendered & Untamed a message heard round the world!

Lee Huff for taking a risk. Everyone at Alive Communications. John Blasé, Chad Allen, and Barb Barnes for the gift of refinement. Everyone at Baker.

Those "Fathers in the Faith" who have influenced me—my dad, Bill Johnson, Kris Vallotton, Graham Cooke, Erwin McManus, Dan Mohler, Dick Grout. We should hang out more as well.

Coldplay, Mumford & Sons, John Mark McMillan, Envy Corps, Anthony Skinner, The Killers, U2, Arcade Fire, Sigur Ros, Brian Johnson, Imogen Heap, Mutemath, Band of a Thousand, The Fire Theft, and many more for the sounds of momentum.

And coffee. Thank you, baristas—you know who you are.

Jason Clark is a published writer with Thomas Nelson for Donald Miller's *The Open Table: An Invitation to Walk with God*. Jason is also a writer for several projects with Switchvert Multimedia that span from commercials and documentaries to sitcom TV programs and film.

An almost-graduate of Elim Bible Institute (1995), Jason has held three worship leadership positions since 1996. He is a recording artist and has released three albums. The first two, *For the Vagabond Believer* and *Sacrifice*, were recorded with his band of seven years, Fringe. His most recent album is entitled *Surrendered & Untamed*. Much of the music from that album is used on the S&U films. Jason's passion is to see a generation step into their identity as sons and daughters of the King and establish His kingdom on earth as it is in heaven.

He is a speaker and worship leader at churches, conferences, and retreats across the country. Jason and his wife, Karen, live in Cornelius, North Carolina, with their three children, Madeleine True, Ethan Wilde, and Eva Blaze.

Permissions

Visit
www.**surrendered**and**untamed**.com
for regularly updated content,
including:

- Excerpts from Alex Harris's video diary

- Video blogs from Mark Batterson,
  Jason Clark, and Alex Harris

- Interactive conversations on faith
  and adventure

- And much more!

Stunning Cinematography and Powerful True Stories Help You Discover a Meaningful and Adventurous Faith

Follow South African extreme explorer Alex Harris on a 65-day, 692-mile unsupported trek across Antarctica. His insightful reflections of faith and adventure will lead you to question and explore your own faith journey.

Whether experienced in a group setting or individually, the combined impact of the participant's guide and DVD will ignite your faith and stir your imagination as it leads you on a journey to the edges of the earth—and the depths of your faith.

a division of Baker Publishing Group
www.BakerBooks.com

Available Wherever Books Are Sold

Many of the song lyrics featured in the book *Surrendered and Untamed* are from Jason Clark's latest album.

This album *Surrendered+Untamed* by Clark
is available on **iTunes** and **Amazon**.

Or check it out at
www.surrenderedanduntamed.com

REVIEWS FOR THE ALBUM *SURRENDERED+UNTAMED* BY CLARK

"It only gets better from there, each track epic in theme and grandeur. Both lyrically and instrumentally, the album is wildly creative and builds an atmosphere of awe that lends itself to sincere worship . . . [This album] will lead you as far into the presence of God as you are willing to go. You can't ask for more than that."

—**Kevan Breitinger**, about.com guest reviewer

"What shines the most on this album is the songwriting. These are great songs; they are songs that mean something. They search, they hope, they fear, they beg for change. This album is simply astounding, don't miss out on it."

—**Mark Fisher**, infuse.cgi.org